PSAT Math for Beginners

The Ultimate Step by Step Guide to Preparing for the PSAT Math Test

By

Reza Nazari

About Effortless Math Education Inc.

Effortless Math Education Inc. operates the www.effortlessmath.com website, which prepares and publishes Test prep and Mathematics learning resources. Effortless Math authors' team strives to prepare and publish the best quality Mathematics learning resources to make learning Math easier for all. We Help Students Learn to Love Mathematics.

All inquiries should be addressed to:
info@EffortlessMath.com
www.EffortlessMath.com

ISBN: 978-1-64612-934-8

Published by: **Effortless Math Education**

for Online Math Practice Visit www.EffortlessMath.com

Welcome to
PSAT Math Prep
2022

Thank you for choosing Effortless Math for your PSAT Math test preparation!

It's a remarkable move you are taking, one that shouldn't be diminished in any capacity. That's why you need to use every tool possible to ensure you succeed on the test with the highest possible score, and this extensive study guide is one such tool.

If math has never been a strong subject for you, **don't worry**! This book will help you prepare for (and even ACE) the PSAT test's math section. As test day draws nearer, effective preparation becomes increasingly more important. Thankfully, you have this comprehensive study guide to help you get ready for the test. With this guide, you can feel confident that you will be more than ready for the PSAT Math test when the time comes.

First and foremost, it is important to note that this book is a study guide and not a textbook. It is best read from cover to cover. Every lesson of this "self-guided math book" was carefully developed to ensure that you are making the most effective use of your time while preparing for the test. This up-to-date guide reflects the 2022 test guidelines and will put you on the right track to hone your math skills, overcome exam anxiety, and boost your confidence, so that you can have your best to succeed on the PSAT Math test.

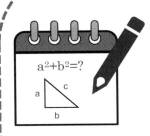

This study guide will:

☑ Explain the format of the PSAT Math test.

☑ Describe specific test-taking strategies that you can use on the test.

☑ Provide PSAT Math test-taking tips.

☑ Review all PSAT Math concepts and topics you will be tested on.

☑ Help you identify the areas in which you need to concentrate your study time.

☑ Offer exercises that help you develop the basic math skills you will learn in each section.

☑ Give **2 realistic and full-length practice tests** (featuring new question types) with detailed answers to help you measure your exam readiness and build confidence.

This resource contains everything you will ever need to succeed on the PSAT Math test. You'll get in-depth instructions on every math topic as well as tips and techniques on how to answer each question type. You'll also get plenty of practice questions to boost your test-taking confidence.

In addition, in the following pages you'll find:

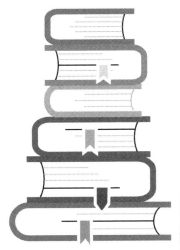

➢ **How to Use This Book Effectively** – This section provides you with step-by-step instructions on how to get the most out of this comprehensive study guide.

➢ **How to study for the PSAT Math Test** – A six-step study program has been developed to help you make the best use of this book and prepare for your PSAT Math test. Here you'll find tips and strategies to guide your study program and help you understand PSAT Math and how to ace the test.

➤ **PSAT Math Review** – Learn everything you need to know about the PSAT Math test.

➤ **PSAT Math Test-Taking Strategies** – Learn how to effectively put these recommended test-taking techniques into use for improving your PSAT Math score.

➤ **Test Day Tips** – Review these tips to make sure you will do your best when the big day comes.

Effortless Math's PSAT Online Center

Effortless Math Online PSAT Center offers a complete study program, including the following:

✓ Step-by-step instructions on how to prepare for the PSAT Math test

✓ Numerous PSAT Math worksheets to help you measure your math skills

✓ Complete list of PSAT Math formulas

✓ Video lessons for all PSAT Math topics

✓ Full-length PSAT Math practice tests

✓ And much more...

No Registration Required.

Visit **EffortlessMath.com/PSAT** to find your online PSAT Math resources.

How to Use This Book Effectively

Look no further when you need a study guide to improve your math skills to succeed on the math portion of the PSAT test. Each chapter of this comprehensive guide to the PSAT Math will provide you with the knowledge, tools, and understanding needed for every topic covered on the test.

It's imperative that you understand each topic before moving onto another one, as that's the way to guarantee your success. Each chapter provides you with examples and a step-by-step guide of every concept to better understand the content that will be on the test. To get the best possible results from this book:

➢ **Begin studying long before your test date.** This provides you ample time to learn the different math concepts. The earlier you begin studying for the test, the sharper your skills will be. Do not procrastinate! Provide yourself with plenty of time to learn the concepts and feel comfortable that you understand them when your test date arrives.

➢ **Practice consistently.** Study PSAT Math concepts at least 20 to 30 minutes a day. Remember, slow and steady wins the race, which can be applied to preparing for the PSAT Math test. Instead of cramming to tackle everything at once, be patient and learn the math topics in short bursts.

➢ Whenever you get a math problem wrong, **mark it off, and review it later** to make sure you understand the concept.

➢ Start each session by **looking over the previous material.**

➢ Once you've reviewed the book's lessons, **take a practice test at the back of the book** to gauge your level of readiness. Then, review your results. Read detailed answers and solutions for each question you missed.

➢ **Take another practice test** to get an idea of how ready you are to take the actual exam. Taking the practice tests will give you the confidence you need on test day. Simulate the PSAT testing environment by sitting in a quiet room free from distraction. Make sure to clock yourself with a timer.

How to Study for the PSAT Math Test

Studying for the PSAT Math test can be a really daunting and boring task. What's the best way to go about it? Is there a certain study method that works better than others? Well, studying for the PSAT Math can be done effectively. The following six-step program has been designed to make preparing for the PSAT Math test more efficient and less overwhelming.

Step **1** - Create a study plan
Step **2** - Choose your study resources
Step **3** - Review, Learn, Practice
Step **4** - Learn and practice test-taking strategies
Step **5** - Learn the PSAT Test format and take practice tests
Step **6** - Analyze your performance

STEP 1: Create a Study Plan

It's always easier to get things done when you have a plan. Creating a study plan for the PSAT Math test can help you to stay on track with your studies. It's important to sit down and prepare a study plan with what works with your life, work, and any other obligations you may have. Devote enough time each day to studying. It's also a great

idea to break down each section of the exam into blocks and study one concept at a time.

It's important to understand that there is no "right" way to create a study plan. Your study plan will be personalized based on your specific needs and learning style.

Follow these guidelines to create an effective study plan for your PSAT Math test:

★ **Analyze your learning style and study habits** – Everyone has a different learning style. It is essential to embrace your individuality and the unique way you learn. Think about what works and what doesn't work for you. Do you prefer PSAT Math prep books or a combination of textbooks and video lessons? Does it work better for you if you study every night for thirty minutes or is it more effective to study in the morning before going to work?

★ **Evaluate your schedule** – Review your current schedule and find out how much time you can consistently devote to PSAT Math study.

★ **Develop a schedule** – Now it's time to add your study schedule to your calendar like any other obligation. Schedule time for study, practice, and review. Plan out which topic you will study on which day to ensure that you're devoting enough time to each concept. Develop a study plan that is mindful, realistic, and flexible.

★ **Stick to your schedule** – A study plan is only effective when it is followed consistently. You should try to develop a study plan that you can follow for the length of your study program.

★ **Evaluate your study plan and adjust as needed** – Sometimes you need to adjust your plan when you have new commitments. Check in with yourself regularly to make sure that you're not falling behind in your study plan. Remember, the most important thing is sticking to your plan. Your study plan is all about helping you be more productive. If you find that your study plan is not as effective as you want, don't get discouraged. It's okay to make changes as you figure out what works best for you.

STEP 2: Choose Your Study Resources

There are numerous textbooks and online resources available for the PSAT Math test, and it may not be clear where to begin. Don't worry! This study guide provides everything you need to fully prepare for your PSAT Math test. In addition to the book content, you can also use Effortless Math's online resources. (video lessons, worksheets, formulas, etc.)

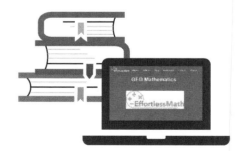

Simply visit EffortlessMath.com/PSAT to find your online PSAT Math resources.

STEP 3: Review, Learn, Practice

This PSAT Math study guide breaks down each subject into specific skills or content areas. For instance, the percent concept is separated into different topics—percent calculation, percent increase and decrease, percent problems, etc. Use this book to help you go over all key math concepts and topics on the PSAT Math test.

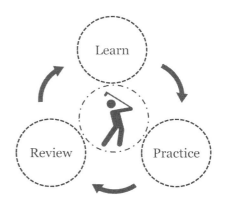

As you read each chapter, take notes or highlight the concepts you would like to go over again in the future. If you're unfamiliar with a topic or something is difficult for you, do additional research on it. For each math topic, plenty of instructions, step-by-step guides, and examples are provided to ensure you get a good grasp of the material. You can also find video lessons on the Effortless Math website for each PSAT Math concept.

Quickly review the topics you do understand to get a brush-up of the material. Be sure to do the practice questions provided at the end of every chapter to measure your understanding of the concepts.

STEP 4: Learn and Practice Test-taking Strategies

In the following sections, you will find important test-taking strategies and tips that can help you earn extra points. You'll learn how to think strategically and when to guess if you don't know the answer to a question. Using PSAT Math test-taking strategies and tips can help you raise your score and do well on the test. Apply test taking strategies on the practice tests to help you boost your confidence.

STEP 5: Learn the PSAT Test Format and Take Practice Tests

The *PSAT Test Review* section provides information about the structure of the PSAT test. Read this section to learn more about the PSAT test structure, different test sections, the number of questions in each section, and the section time limits. When you have a prior understanding of the test format and different types of PSAT Math questions, you'll feel more confident when you take the actual exam.

Once you have read through the instructions and lessons and feel like you are ready to go – take advantage of both of the full-length PSAT Math practice tests available in this study guide. Use the practice tests to sharpen your skills and build confidence.

The PSAT Math practice tests offered at the end of the book are formatted similarly to the actual PSAT Math test. When you take each practice test, try to simulate actual testing conditions. To take the practice tests, sit in a quiet space, time yourself, and work through as many of the questions as time allows. The practice tests are followed by detailed answer explanations to help you find your weak areas, learn from your mistakes, and raise your PSAT Math score.

STEP 6: Analyze Your Performance

After taking the practice tests, look over the answer keys and explanations to learn which questions you answered correctly and which you did not. Never be discouraged if you make a few mistakes. See them as a learning opportunity. This will highlight your strengths and weaknesses.

You can use the results to determine if you need additional practice or if you are ready to take the actual PSAT Math test.

Looking for more?

Visit EffortlessMath.com/PSAT to find hundreds of PSAT Math worksheets, video tutorials, practice tests, PSAT Math formulas, and much more.

Or scan this QR code.

No Registration Required.

PSAT Test Review

The Preliminary SAT/ National Merit Scholarship Qualifying Test (PSAT/NMSQT) is a standardized test used for college admissions in the United States. 10th and 11th graders take the PSAT to practice for the SAT and to secure a National Merit distinction or scholarship.

The PSAT is similar to the SAT in both format and content. There are three sections on the PSAT:

- Reading
- Math
- Writing

The PSAT Math section is divided into two subsections:

A **No Calculator Section** contains 17 questions and students cannot use a calculator. Students have 25 minutes to complete this section.

A **Calculator Section** contains 31 questions. Students have 45 minutes to complete this section.

40 questions are multiple choice questions and 8 questions are grid-ins.

PSAT Math cover the following topics:

- Pre-Algebra
- Algebra
- Coordinate Geometry
- Plane Geometry
- Date analysis and basic Statistics
- Trigonometry

PSAT Math Test-Taking Strategies

Here are some test-taking strategies that you can use to maximize your performance and results on the PSAT Math test.

#1 : USE THIS APPROACH TO ANSWER EVERY PSAT MATH QUESTION

- Review the question to identify keywords and important information.
- Translate the keywords into math operations so you can solve the problem.
- Review the answer choices. What are the differences between answer choices?
- Draw or label a diagram if needed.
- Try to find patterns.
- Find the right method to answer the question. Use straightforward math, plug in numbers, or test the answer choices (backsolving).
- Double-check your work.

#2 : USE EDUCATED GUESSING

This approach is applicable to the problems you understand to some degree but cannot solve using straightforward math. In such cases, try to filter out as many answer choices as possible before picking an answer. In cases where you don't have a clue about what a certain problem entails, don't waste any time trying to eliminate answer choices. Just choose one randomly before moving onto the next question.

As you can ascertain, direct solutions are the most optimal approach. Carefully read through the question, determine what the solution is using the math you have learned before, then coordinate the answer with one of the choices available to you. Are you stumped? Make your best guess, then move on.

Don't leave any fields empty! Even if you're unable to work out a problem, strive to answer it. Take a guess if you have to. You will not lose points by getting an answer wrong, though you may gain a point by getting it correct!

#3: BALLPARK

A ballpark answer is a rough approximation. When we become overwhelmed by calculations and figures, we end up making silly mistakes. A decimal that is moved by one unit can change an answer from right to wrong, regardless of the number of steps that you went through to get it. That's where ballparking can play a big part.

If you think you know what the correct answer may be (even if it's just a ballpark answer), you'll usually have the ability to eliminate a couple of choices. While answer choices are usually based on the average student error and/or values that are closely tied, you will still be able to weed out choices that are way far afield. Try to find answers that aren't in the proverbial ballpark when you're looking for a wrong answer on a multiple-choice question. This is an optimal approach to eliminating answers to a problem.

#4: BACKSOLVING

A majority of questions on the PSAT Math test will be in multiple-choice format. Many test-takers prefer multiple-choice questions, as at least the answer is right there. You'll typically have four answers to pick from. You simply need to figure out which one is correct. Usually, the best way to go about doing so is "backsolving."

As mentioned earlier, direct solutions are the most optimal approach to answering a question. Carefully read through a problem, calculate a solution, then correspond the answer with one of the choices displayed in front of you. If you can't calculate a solution, your next best approach involves "backsolving."

When backsolving a problem, contrast one of your answer options against the problem you are asked, then see which of them is most relevant. More often than not, answer choices are listed in ascending or descending order. In such cases, try out the choices B or C. If it's not correct, you can go either down or up from there.

#5 : PLUGGING IN NUMBERS

"Plugging in numbers" is a strategy that can be applied to a wide range of different math problems on the PSAT Math test. This approach is typically used to simplify a challenging question so that it is more understandable. By using the strategy carefully, you can find the answer without too much trouble.

The concept is fairly straightforward–replace unknown variables in a problem with certain values. When selecting a number, consider the following:

- Choose a number that's basic (just not too basic). Generally, you should avoid choosing 1 (or even 0). A decent choice is 2.

- Try not to choose a number that is displayed in the problem.

- Make sure you keep your numbers different if you need to choose at least two of them.

- More often than not, choosing numbers merely lets you filter out some of your answer choices. As such, don't just go with the first choice that gives you the right answer.

- If several answers seem correct, then you'll need to choose another value and try again. This time, though, you'll just need to check choices that haven't been eliminated yet.

- If your question contains fractions, then a potential right answer may involve either an LCD (least common denominator) or an LCD multiple.

- 100 is the number you should choose when you are dealing with problems involving percentages.

PSAT Mathematics Test – Daytime Tips

After practicing and reviewing all the math concepts you've been taught, and taking some PSAT mathematics practice tests, you'll be prepared for test day. Consider the following tips to be extra-ready come test time.

Before Your Test

What to do the night before:

- **Relax!** One day before your test, study lightly or skip studying altogether. You shouldn't attempt to learn something new, either. There are plenty of reasons why studying the evening before a big test can work against you. Put it this way–a marathoner wouldn't go out for a sprint before the day of a big race. Mental marathoners–such as yourself–should not study for any more than one hour 24 hours before a PSAT test. That's because your brain requires some rest to be at its best. The night before your exam, spend some time with family or friends, or read a book.

- **Avoid bright screens** - You'll have to get some good shuteye the night before your test. Bright screens (such as the ones coming from your laptop, TV, or mobile device) should be avoided altogether. Staring at such a screen will keep your brain up, making it hard to drift asleep at a reasonable hour.

- **Make sure your dinner is healthy** - The meal that you have for dinner should be nutritious. Be sure to drink plenty of water as well. Load up on your complex carbohydrates, much like a marathon runner would do. Pasta, rice, and potatoes are ideal options here, as are vegetables and protein sources.

- **Get your bag ready for test day** - The night prior to your test, pack your bag with your stationery, admissions pass, ID, calculator, and any other gear that you need. Keep the bag right by your front door.

- **Make plans to reach the testing site** - Before going to sleep, ensure that you understand precisely how you will arrive at the site of the test. If parking is something you'll have to find first, plan for it. If you're dependent on public transit, then review the schedule. You should also make sure that the train/bus/subway/streetcar you use will be running. Find out about road

closures as well. If a parent or friend is accompanying you, ensure that they understand what steps they have to take as well.

The Day of the Test

- **Get up reasonably early, but not too early.**

- **Have breakfast** - Breakfast improves your concentration, memory, and mood. As such, make sure the breakfast that you eat in the morning is healthy. The last thing you want to be is distracted by a grumbling tummy. If it's not your own stomach making those noises, another test taker close to you might be instead. Prevent discomfort or embarrassment by consuming a healthy breakfast. Bring a snack with you if you think you'll need it.

- **Follow your daily routine** - Don't break your usual habits on the day of the test. Likewise, if coffee isn't something you drink in the morning, then don't take up the habit hours before your test. Routine consistency lets you concentrate on the main objective–doing the best you can on your test.

- **Wear layers** - Dress yourself up in comfortable layers. You should be ready for any kind of internal temperature. If it gets too warm during the test, take a layer off.

- **Get there on time** - The last thing you want to do is get to the test site late. Rather, you should be there 45 minutes prior to the start of the test. Upon your arrival, try not to hang out with anybody who is nervous. Any anxious energy they exhibit shouldn't influence you.

- **Leave the books at home** - No books should be brought to the test site. If you start developing anxiety before the test, books could encourage you to do some last-minute studying, which will only hinder you. Keep the books far away–better yet, leave them at home.

- **Make your voice heard** - If something is off, speak to a proctor. If medical attention is needed or if you'll require anything, consult the proctor prior to the start of the test. Any doubts you have should be clarified. You should be entering the test site with a state of mind that is completely clear.

- **Have faith in yourself** - When you feel confident, you will be able to perform at your best. When you are waiting for the test to begin, envision yourself receiving an outstanding result. Try to see yourself as someone who knows all the answers, no matter what the questions are. A lot of athletes tend to use this technique–particularly before a big competition. Your expectations will be reflected by your performance.

During your test

- **Be calm and breathe deeply** - You need to relax before the test, and some deep breathing will go a long way to help you do that. Be confident and calm. You got this. Everybody feels a little stressed out just before an evaluation of any kind is set to begin. Learn some effective breathing exercises. Spend a minute meditating before the test starts. Filter out any negative thoughts you have. Exhibit confidence when having such thoughts.

- **Concentrate on the test** - Refrain from comparing yourself to anyone else. You shouldn't be distracted by the people near you or random noise. Concentrate exclusively on the test. If you find yourself irritated by surrounding noises, earplugs can be used to block sounds off close to you. Don't forget–the test is going to last several hours if you're taking more than one subject of the test. Some of that time will be dedicated to brief sections. Concentrate on the specific section you are working on during a particular moment. Do not let your mind wander off to upcoming or previous sections.

- **Skip challenging questions** - Optimize your time when taking the test. Lingering on a single question for too long will work against you. If you don't know what the answer is to a certain question, use your best guess, and mark the question so you can review it later on. There is no need to spend time attempting to solve something you aren't sure about. That time would be better served handling the questions you can actually answer well. You will not be penalized for getting the wrong answer on a test like this.

- **Try to answer each question individually** - Focus only on the question you are working on. Use one of the test-taking strategies to solve the problem. If you aren't able to come up with an answer, don't get frustrated. Simply skip that question, then move onto the next one.

- **Don't forget to breathe!** Whenever you notice your mind wandering, your stress levels boosting, or frustration brewing, take a thirty-second break. Shut your eyes, drop your pencil, breathe deeply, and let your shoulders relax. You will end up being more productive when you allow yourself to relax for a moment.

- **Review your answer.** If you still have time at the end of the test, don't waste it. Go back and check over your answers. It is worth going through the test from start to finish to ensure that you didn't make a sloppy mistake somewhere.

- **Optimize your breaks** - When break time comes, use the restroom, have a snack, and reactivate your energy for the subsequent section. Doing some stretches can help stimulate your blood flow.

After your test

- **Take it easy** - You will need to set some time aside to relax and decompress once the test has concluded. There is no need to stress yourself out about what you could've said, or what you may have done wrong. At this point, there's nothing you can do about it. Your energy and time would be better spent on something that will bring you happiness for the remainder of your day.

- **Redoing the test** - Did you succeed on the test? Congratulations! Your hard work paid off!

  If you didn't get the result you expected, though, don't worry! You can take the SAT test in the future.

Contents

Chapter: **Trigonometric Functions** 177

19

1 Fractions and Mixed Numbers

Math topics that you'll learn in this chapter:

- ☑ Simplifying Fractions
- ☑ Adding and Subtracting Fractions
- ☑ Multiplying and Dividing Fractions
- ☑ Adding Mixed Numbers
- ☑ Subtracting Mixed Numbers
- ☑ Multiplying Mixed Numbers
- ☑ Dividing Mixed Numbers

1

Simplifying Fractions

- A fraction contains two numbers separated by a bar between them. The bottom number, called the denominator, is the total number of equally divided portions in one whole. The top number, called the numerator, is how many portions you have. And the bar represents the operation of division.

- Simplifying a fraction means reducing it to the lowest terms. To simplify a fraction, evenly divide both the top and bottom of the fraction by $2, 3, 5, 7$, etc.

- Continue until you can't go any further.

Examples:

Example 1. Simplify $\frac{18}{30}$

Solution: To simplify $\frac{18}{30}$, find a number that both 18 and 30 are divisible by. Both are divisible by 6. Then: $\frac{18}{30} = \frac{18 \div 6}{30 \div 6} = \frac{3}{5}$

Example 2. Simplify $\frac{48}{80}$

Solution: To simplify $\frac{48}{80}$, find a number that both 48 and 80 are divisible by. Both are divisible by 8 and 16. Then: $\frac{48}{80} = \frac{48 \div 8}{80 \div 8} = \frac{6}{10}$, 6 and 10 are divisible by 2, then: $\frac{6}{10} = \frac{3}{5}$ or $\frac{48}{80} = \frac{48 \div 16}{80 \div 16} = \frac{3}{5}$

Example 3. Simplify $\frac{40}{120}$

Solution: To simplify $\frac{40}{120}$, find a number that both 40 and 120 are divisible by. Both are divisible by 40, then: $\frac{40}{120} = \frac{40 \div 40}{120 \div 40} = \frac{1}{3}$

bit.ly/3nOGNko

Find more at

Adding and Subtracting Fractions

- For "like" fractions (fractions with the same denominator), add or subtract the numerators (top numbers) and write the answer over the common denominator (bottom numbers).

- Adding and Subtracting fractions with the same denominator:

$$- \frac{a}{b} + \frac{c}{b} = \frac{a+c}{b} \qquad \frac{a}{b} - \frac{c}{b} = \frac{a-c}{b}$$

- Find equivalent fractions with the same denominator before you can add or subtract fractions with different denominators.

- Adding and Subtracting fractions with different denominators:

$$\frac{a}{b} + \frac{c}{d} = \frac{ad+bc}{bd} \qquad \frac{a}{b} - \frac{c}{d} = \frac{ad-bc}{bd}$$

Examples:

Example 1. Find the sum. $\frac{2}{3} + \frac{1}{2} =$

Solution: These two fractions are "unlike" fractions. (they have different denominators). Use this formula: $\frac{a}{b} + \frac{c}{d} = \frac{ad+cb}{bd}$

Then: $\frac{2}{3} + \frac{1}{2} = \frac{(2)(2)+(3)(1)}{3 \times 2} = \frac{4+3}{6} = \frac{7}{6}$

Example 2. Find the difference. $\frac{3}{5} - \frac{2}{7} =$

Solution: For "unlike" fractions, find equivalent fractions with the same denominator before you can add or subtract fractions with different denominators. Use this formula:

$\frac{a}{b} - \frac{c}{d} = \frac{ad-bc}{bd}$

$\frac{3}{5} - \frac{2}{7} = \frac{(3)(7)-(2)(5)}{5 \times 7} = \frac{21-10}{35} = \frac{11}{35}$

Multiplying and Dividing Fractions

- Multiplying fractions: multiply the top numbers and multiply the bottom numbers. Simplify if necessary. $\frac{a}{b} \times \frac{c}{d} = \frac{a \times c}{b \times d}$

- Dividing fractions: Keep, Change, Flip

- Keep the first fraction, change the division sign to multiplication, and flip the numerator and denominator of the second fraction. Then, solve!

$$\frac{a}{b} \div \frac{c}{d} = \frac{a}{b} \times \frac{d}{c} = \frac{a \times d}{b \times c}$$

Examples:

Example 1. Multiply. $\frac{2}{3} \times \frac{3}{5} =$

Solution: Multiply the top numbers and multiply the bottom numbers.
$\frac{2}{3} \times \frac{3}{5} = \frac{2 \times 3}{3 \times 5} = \frac{6}{15}$

Example 2. Solve. $\frac{3}{4} \div \frac{2}{5} =$

Solution: Keep the first fraction, change the division sign to multiplication, and flip the numerator and denominator of the second fraction.
Then: $\frac{3}{4} \div \frac{2}{5} = \frac{3}{4} \times \frac{5}{2} = \frac{3 \times 5}{4 \times 2} = \frac{15}{8}$

Example 3. Calculate. $\frac{4}{5} \times \frac{3}{4} =$

Solution: Multiply the top numbers and multiply the bottom numbers.
$\frac{4}{5} \times \frac{3}{4} = \frac{4 \times 3}{5 \times 4} = \frac{12}{20}$, simplify: $\frac{12}{20} = \frac{12 \div 4}{20 \div 4} = \frac{3}{5}$

Example 4. Solve. $\frac{5}{6} \div \frac{3}{7} =$

Solution: Keep the first fraction, change the division sign to multiplication, and flip the numerator and denominator of the second fraction.
Then: $\frac{5}{6} \div \frac{3}{7} = \frac{5}{6} \times \frac{7}{3} = \frac{5 \times 7}{6 \times 3} = \frac{35}{18}$

Adding Mixed Numbers

Use the following steps for adding mixed numbers:

- Add whole numbers of the mixed numbers.

- Add the fractions of the mixed numbers.

- Find the Least Common Denominator (LCD) if necessary.

- Add whole numbers and fractions.

- Write your answer in lowest terms.

Examples:

Example 1. Add mixed numbers. $2\frac{1}{2} + 1\frac{2}{3} =$

Solution: Let's rewriting our equation with parts separated, $2\frac{1}{2} + 1\frac{2}{3} = 2 + \frac{1}{2} + 1 + \frac{2}{3}$. Now, add whole number parts: $2 + 1 = 3$

Add the fraction parts $\frac{1}{2} + \frac{2}{3}$. Rewrite to solve with the equivalent fractions. $\frac{1}{2} + \frac{2}{3} = \frac{3}{6} + \frac{4}{6} = \frac{7}{6}$. The answer is an improper fraction (numerator is bigger than denominator). Convert the improper fraction into a mixed number: $\frac{7}{6} = 1\frac{1}{6}$. Now, combine the whole and fraction parts: $3 + 1\frac{1}{6} = 4\frac{1}{6}$

Example 2. Find the sum. $1\frac{3}{4} + 2\frac{1}{2} =$

Solution: Rewriting our equation with parts separated, $1 + \frac{3}{4} + 2 + \frac{1}{2}$. Add the whole number parts:

$1 + 2 = 3$. Add the fraction parts: $\frac{3}{4} + \frac{1}{2} = \frac{3}{4} + \frac{2}{4} = \frac{5}{4}$

Convert the improper fraction into a mixed number: $\frac{5}{4} = 1\frac{1}{4}$.

Now, combine the whole and fraction parts: $3 + 1\frac{1}{4} = 4\frac{1}{4}$

bit.ly/2M4oABB

Find more at

Subtracting Mixed Numbers

Use these steps for subtracting mixed numbers.

- Convert mixed numbers into improper fractions. $a\frac{c}{b} = \frac{ab+c}{b}$

- Find equivalent fractions with the same denominator for unlike fractions. (fractions with different denominators)

- Subtract the second fraction from the first one. $\frac{a}{b} - \frac{c}{d} = \frac{ad-bc}{bd}$

- Write your answer in lowest terms.

- If the answer is an improper fraction, convert it into a mixed number.

Examples:

Example 1. Subtract. $2\frac{1}{3} - 1\frac{1}{2} =$

Solution: Convert mixed numbers into fractions: $2\frac{1}{3} = \frac{2\times3+1}{3} = \frac{7}{3}$ and $1\frac{1}{2} = \frac{1\times2+1}{2} = \frac{3}{2}$

These two fractions are "unlike" fractions. (they have different denominators). Find equivalent fractions with the same denominator. Use this formula: $\frac{a}{b} - \frac{c}{d} = \frac{ad-bc}{bd}$

$\frac{7}{3} - \frac{3}{2} = \frac{(7)(2)-(3)(3)}{3\times2} = \frac{14-9}{6} = \frac{5}{6}$

Example 2. Subtract. $3\frac{4}{7} - 2\frac{3}{4} =$

Solution: Convert mixed numbers into fractions: $3\frac{4}{7} = \frac{3\times7+4}{7} = \frac{25}{7}$ and $2\frac{3}{4} = \frac{2\times4+3}{4} = \frac{11}{4}$

Then: $3\frac{4}{7} - 2\frac{3}{4} = \frac{25}{7} - \frac{11}{4} = \frac{(25)(4)-(11)(7)}{7\times4} = \frac{23}{28}$

Multiplying Mixed Numbers

Use the following steps for multiplying mixed numbers:

- Convert the mixed numbers into fractions. $a\frac{c}{b} = a + \frac{c}{b} = \frac{ab+c}{b}$

- Multiply fractions. $\frac{a}{b} \times \frac{c}{d} = \frac{a \times c}{b \times d}$

- Write your answer in lowest terms.

- If the answer is an improper fraction (numerator is bigger than denominator), convert it into a mixed number.

Examples:

Example 1. Multiply. $4\frac{1}{2} \times 2\frac{2}{5} =$

Solution: Convert mixed numbers into fractions, $4\frac{1}{2} = \frac{4 \times 2 + 1}{2} = \frac{9}{2}$ and

$$2\frac{2}{5} = \frac{2 \times 5 + 2}{5} = \frac{12}{5}$$

Apply the fractions rule for multiplication, $\frac{9}{2} \times \frac{12}{5} = \frac{9 \times 12}{2 \times 5} = \frac{108}{10}$

The answer is an improper fraction. Convert it into a mixed number. $\frac{108}{10} = 10\frac{4}{5}$

Example 2. Multiply. $3\frac{2}{3} \times 2\frac{5}{6} =$

Solution: Converting mixed numbers into fractions, $3\frac{2}{3} \times 2\frac{5}{6} = \frac{11}{3} \times \frac{17}{6}$

Apply the fractions rule for multiplication, $\frac{11}{3} \times \frac{17}{6} = \frac{11 \times 17}{3 \times 6} = \frac{187}{18} = 10\frac{7}{18}$

Example 3. Multiply mixed numbers. $5\frac{1}{4} \times 3\frac{3}{8} =$

Solution: Converting mixed numbers to fractions, $5\frac{1}{4} = \frac{21}{4}$ and $3\frac{3}{8} = \frac{27}{8}$. Multiply

two fractions:

$\frac{21}{4} \times \frac{27}{8} = \frac{21 \times 27}{4 \times 8} = \frac{567}{32} = 17\frac{23}{32}$

bit.ly/3aPy7XJ

Find more at

Dividing Mixed Numbers

Use the following steps for dividing mixed numbers:

- Convert the mixed numbers into fractions. $a\frac{c}{b} = a + \frac{c}{b} = \frac{ab+c}{b}$

- Divide fractions: Keep, Change, Flip: Keep the first fraction, change the division sign to multiplication, and flip the numerator and denominator of the second fraction. Then, solve! $\frac{a}{b} \div \frac{c}{d} = \frac{a}{b} \times \frac{d}{c} = \frac{a \times d}{b \times c}$

- Write your answer in lowest terms.

- If the answer is an improper fraction (numerator is bigger than denominator), convert it into a mixed number.

Examples:

Example 1. Solve. $2\frac{1}{3} \div 1\frac{1}{2}$

Solution: Convert mixed numbers into fractions: $2\frac{1}{3} = \frac{2 \times 3 + 1}{3} = \frac{7}{3}$ and $1\frac{1}{2} = \frac{1 \times 2 + 1}{2} = \frac{3}{2}$
Keep, Change, Flip: $\frac{7}{3} \div \frac{3}{2} = \frac{7}{3} \times \frac{2}{3} = \frac{7 \times 2}{3 \times 3} = \frac{14}{9}$. The answer is an improper fraction. Convert it into a mixed number: $\frac{14}{9} = 1\frac{5}{9}$

Example 2. Solve. $3\frac{3}{4} \div 2\frac{2}{5}$

Solution: Convert mixed numbers to fractions, then solve:
$3\frac{3}{4} \div 2\frac{2}{5} = \frac{15}{4} \div \frac{12}{5} = \frac{15}{4} \times \frac{5}{12} = \frac{75}{48} = 1\frac{9}{16}$

Example 3. Solve. $2\frac{4}{5} \div 1\frac{2}{3}$

Solution: Converting mixed numbers to fractions: $2\frac{4}{5} \div 1\frac{2}{3} = \frac{14}{5} \div \frac{5}{3}$
Keep, Change, Flip: $\frac{14}{5} \div \frac{5}{3} = \frac{14}{5} \times \frac{3}{5} = \frac{14 \times 3}{5 \times 5} = \frac{42}{25} = 1\frac{17}{25}$

Chapter 1: Practices

✍ Simplify each fraction.

1) $\frac{2}{8} =$

2) $\frac{5}{15} =$

3) $\frac{10}{90} =$

4) $\frac{12}{16} =$

5) $\frac{25}{45} =$

6) $\frac{42}{54} =$

7) $\frac{48}{60} =$

8) $\frac{52}{169} =$

✍ Find the sum or difference.

9) $\frac{3}{10} + \frac{2}{10} =$

10) $\frac{4}{9} - \frac{1}{9} =$

11) $\frac{2}{3} + \frac{6}{15} =$

12) $\frac{17}{24} - \frac{5}{8} =$

13) $\frac{7}{54} - \frac{1}{9} =$

14) $\frac{4}{5} - \frac{1}{6} =$

15) $\frac{6}{7} - \frac{3}{8} =$

16) $\frac{2}{13} + \frac{1}{4} =$

✍ Find the products or quotients.

17) $\frac{2}{9} \div \frac{4}{3} =$

18) $\frac{14}{5} \div \frac{28}{35} =$

19) $\frac{9}{25} \times \frac{5}{27} =$

20) $\frac{65}{72} \times \frac{12}{15} =$

✍ Find the sum.

21) $2\frac{1}{5} + 1\frac{2}{5} =$

22) $5\frac{1}{9} + 2\frac{7}{9} =$

23) $2\frac{3}{4} + 1\frac{1}{8} =$

24) $2\frac{2}{7} + 4\frac{1}{21} =$

25) $5\frac{3}{5} + 1\frac{4}{9} =$

26) $3\frac{3}{11} + 4\frac{6}{7} =$

Effortless
Math
Education

✎ Find the difference.

27) $5\frac{1}{3} - 4\frac{2}{3} =$

28) $4\frac{7}{10} - 1\frac{3}{10} =$

29) $3\frac{1}{3} - 2\frac{2}{9} =$

30) $6\frac{1}{2} - 3\frac{1}{3} =$

31) $4\frac{3}{4} - 2\frac{1}{28} =$

32) $4\frac{2}{7} - 3\frac{1}{6} =$

33) $5\frac{3}{10} - 3\frac{3}{4} =$

34) $6\frac{9}{20} - 2\frac{1}{3} =$

✎ Find the products.

35) $1\frac{1}{2} \times 2\frac{3}{7} =$

36) $1\frac{3}{4} \times 1\frac{3}{5} =$

37) $4\frac{1}{2} \times 1\frac{5}{6} =$

38) $1\frac{2}{7} \times 3\frac{1}{5} =$

39) $2\frac{1}{5} \times 5\frac{1}{2} =$

40) $2\frac{1}{2} \times 4\frac{4}{5} =$

41) $3\frac{1}{5} \times 4\frac{1}{2} =$

42) $4\frac{9}{10} \times 4\frac{1}{2} =$

✎ Solve.

43) $1\frac{1}{3} \div 1\frac{2}{3} =$

44) $2\frac{1}{4} \div 1\frac{1}{2} =$

45) $5\frac{1}{3} \div 3\frac{1}{2} =$

46) $3\frac{2}{7} \div 1\frac{1}{8} =$

47) $4\frac{1}{5} \div 2\frac{2}{3} =$

48) $1\frac{2}{3} \div 1\frac{3}{8} =$

49) $4\frac{1}{2} \div 2\frac{2}{3} =$

50) $1\frac{2}{11} \div 1\frac{1}{8} =$

Effortless Math Education

Effortless
Math
Education

Chapter 1: Answers

1) $\frac{1}{4}$

2) $\frac{1}{3}$

3) $\frac{1}{9}$

4) $\frac{3}{4}$

5) $\frac{5}{9}$

6) $\frac{7}{9}$

7) $\frac{4}{5}$

8) $\frac{4}{13}$

9) $\frac{1}{2}$

10) $\frac{1}{3}$

11) $\frac{16}{15} = 1\frac{1}{15}$

12) $\frac{1}{12}$

13) $\frac{1}{54}$

14) $\frac{19}{30}$

15) $\frac{27}{56}$

16) $\frac{21}{52}$

17) $\frac{1}{6}$

18) $\frac{7}{2} = 3\frac{1}{2}$

19) $\frac{1}{15}$

20) $\frac{13}{18}$

21) $3\frac{3}{5}$

22) $7\frac{8}{9}$

23) $3\frac{7}{8}$

24) $6\frac{1}{3}$

25) $7\frac{2}{45}$

26) $8\frac{10}{77}$

27) $\frac{2}{3}$

28) $3\frac{2}{5}$

29) $1\frac{1}{9}$

30) $3\frac{1}{6}$

31) $2\frac{5}{7}$

32) $1\frac{5}{42}$

33) $1\frac{11}{20}$

34) $4\frac{7}{60}$

35) $3\frac{9}{14}$

36) $2\frac{4}{5}$

37) $8\frac{1}{4}$

38) $4\frac{4}{35}$

39) $12\frac{1}{10}$

40) 12

41) $14\frac{2}{5}$

42) $22\frac{1}{20}$

43) $\frac{4}{5}$

44) $1\frac{1}{2}$

45) $1\frac{11}{21}$

46) $2\frac{58}{63}$

47) $1\frac{23}{40}$

48) $1\frac{7}{33}$

49) $1\frac{11}{16}$

50) $1\frac{5}{99}$

Effortless
Math
Education

2 Decimals

Math topics that you'll learn in this chapter:

- ☑ Comparing Decimals
- ☑ Rounding Decimals
- ☑ Adding and Subtracting Decimals
- ☑ Multiplying and Dividing Decimals

13

Comparing Decimals

- A decimal is a fraction written in a special form. For example, instead of writing $\frac{1}{2}$ you can write 0.5

- A Decimal Number contains a Decimal Point. It separates the whole number part from the fractional part of a decimal number.

- Let's review decimal place values: Example: **53.9861**

     5: tens   3: ones   9: tenths

     8: hundredths   6: thousandths   1: tens thousandths

- To compare decimals, compare each digit of two decimals in the same place value. Start from left. Compare hundreds, tens, ones, tenth, hundredth, etc.

- To compare numbers, use these symbols:

     Equal to =,   Less than <,   Greater than >

     Greater than or equal ≥,   Less than or equal ≤

Examples:

Example 1. Compare 0.03 and 0.30.

Solution: 0.30 *is greater than* 0.03, because the tenth place of 0.30 is 3, but the tenth place of 0.03 is zero. Then: 0.03 < 0.30

Example 2. Compare 0.0217 and 0.217.

Solution: 0.217 *is greater than* 0.0217, because the tenth place of 0.217 is 2, but the tenth place of 0.0217 is zero. Then: 0.0217 < 0.217

Rounding Decimals

- We can round decimals to a certain accuracy or number of decimal places. This is used to make calculations easier to do and results easier to understand when exact values are not too important.

- First, you'll need to remember your place values: For example: **12.4869**

    1: tens   2: ones   4: tenths

    8: hundredths   6: thousandths   9: tens thousandths

- To round a decimal, first find the place value you'll round to.

- Find the digit to the right of the place value you're rounding to. If it is 5 or bigger, add 1 to the place value you're rounding to and remove all digits on its right side. If the digit to the right of the place value is less than 5, keep the place value and remove all digits on the right.

Examples:

Example 1. Round 4.3679 to the thousandth place value.

Solution: First, look at the next place value to the right, (tens thousandths). It's 9 and it is greater than 5. Thus add 1 to the digit in the thousandth place. The thousandth place is 7. $\rightarrow 7 + 1 = 8$, then,
The answer is 4.368

Example 2. Round 1.5237 to the nearest hundredth.

Solution: First, look at the digit to the right of hundredth (thousandths place value). It's 3 and it is less than 5, thus remove all the digits to the right of hundredth place. Then, the answer is 1.52

Adding and Subtracting Decimals

- Line up the decimal numbers.

- Add zeros to have the same number of digits for both numbers if necessary.

- Remember your place values: For example: 73.5196

    7: tens   3: ones   5: tenths

    1: hundredths   9: thousandths   6: tens thousandths

- Add or subtract using column addition or subtraction.

Examples:

Example 1. Add. $1.7 + 4.12$

Solution: First, line up the numbers: $\begin{array}{r} 1.7 \\ + 4.12 \\ \hline \end{array} \rightarrow$ Add a zero to have the same number of digits for both numbers. $\begin{array}{r} 1.70 \\ + 4.12 \\ \hline \end{array} \rightarrow$ Start with the hundredths place: $0 + 2 = 2,$ $\begin{array}{r} 1.70 \\ + 4.12 \\ \hline 2 \end{array} \rightarrow$ Continue with tenths place: $7 + 1 = 8,$ $\begin{array}{r} 1.70 \\ + 4.12 \\ \hline .82 \end{array} \rightarrow$ Add the ones place: $4 + 1 = 5,$ $\begin{array}{r} 1.70 \\ + 4.12 \\ \hline 5.82 \end{array}$

Example 2. Find the difference. $5.58 - 4.23$

Solution: First, line up the numbers: $\begin{array}{r} 5.58 \\ - 4.23 \\ \hline \end{array} \rightarrow$ Start with the hundredths place: $8 - 3 = 5,$ $\begin{array}{r} 5.58 \\ - 4.23 \\ \hline 5 \end{array} \rightarrow$ Continue with tenths place. $5 - 2 = 3,$ $\begin{array}{r} 5.58 \\ - 4.23 \\ \hline .35 \end{array} \rightarrow$ Subtract the ones place. $5 - 4 = 1,$ $\begin{array}{r} 5.58 \\ - 4.23 \\ \hline 1.35 \end{array}$

Multiplying and Dividing Decimals

For multiplying decimals:

- Ignore the decimal point and set up and multiply the numbers as you do with whole numbers.

- Count the total number of decimal places in both of the factors.

- Place the decimal point in the product.

For dividing decimals:

- If the divisor is not a whole number, move the decimal point to the right to make it a whole number. Do the same for the dividend.

- Divide similar to whole numbers.

Examples:

Example 1. Find the product. $0.65 \times 0.24 =$

Solution: Set up and multiply the numbers as you do with whole numbers. Line up the numbers: $\begin{array}{r} 65 \\ \times 24 \\ \hline \end{array}$ → Start with the ones place then continue with other digits $\rightarrow \begin{array}{r} 65 \\ \times 24 \\ \hline 1,560 \end{array}$. Count the total number of decimal places in both of the factors. There are four decimals digits. (two for each factor 0.65 and 0.24) Then: $0.65 \times 0.24 = 0.1560$

Example 2. Find the quotient. $1.20 \div 0.4 =$

Solution: The divisor is not a whole number. Multiply it by 10 to get 4: → $0.4 \times 10 = 4$
Do the same for the dividend to get 12. → $1.20 \times 10 = 12$
Now, divide $12 \div 4 = 3$. The answer is 3.

bit.ly/34DZ0cS
Find more at

Chapter 2: Practices

✍ Compare. Use >, =, and <

1) 0.5 ☐ 0.6

2) 0.9 ☐ 0.8

3) 0.1 ☐ 0.2

4) 0.02 ☐ 0.06

5) 0.05 ☐ 0.08

6) 0.12 ☐ 0.09

7) 3.2 ☐ 2.5

8) 4.8 ☐ 8.4

9) 0.005 ☐ 0.05

10) 2.02 ☐ 20.020

11) 55.100 ☐ 55.10

12) 0.44 ☐ 0.440

13) 6.01 ☐ 6.0100

14) 0.77 ☐ 77.0

✍ Round each decimal to the nearest whole number.

15) 5.8

16) 6.4

17) 12.3

18) 9.2

19) 7.6

20) 22.4

21) 6.8

22) 15.9

23) 13.41

24) 16.78

25) 67.58

26) 42.67

27) 55.89

28) 14.32

29) 78.88

30) 98.29

Effortless
Math
Education

✍ Find the sum or difference.

31) $12.1 + 36.2 =$

32) $56.3 - 22.2 =$

33) $45.1 + 12.8 =$

34) $27.9 - 16.4 =$

35) $98.8 - 56.6 =$

36) $28.45 + 13.22 =$

37) $16.78 + 45.11 =$

38) $86.16 - 72.12 =$

39) $96.23 - 28.32 =$

40) $57.33 + 67.46 =$

41) $46.26 - 39.49 =$

42) $44.95 + 76.53 =$

43) $79.37 - 52.89 =$

44) $19.99 + 28.7 =$

45) $83.48 - 49.3 =$

46) $19.6 + 42.98 =$

✍ Find the product or quotient.

47) $3.3 \times 0.2 =$

48) $2.4 \div 0.3 =$

49) $8.1 \times 1.4 =$

50) $4.8 \div 0.2 =$

51) $4.1 \times 0.3 =$

52) $8.6 \div 0.2 =$

53) $9.9 \times 0.8 =$

54) $1.84 \div 0.2 =$

55) $2.1 \times 8.4 =$

56) $1.6 \times 4.5 =$

57) $9.2 \times 3.1 =$

58) $36.6 \div 1.6 =$

59) $1.91 \times 5.2 =$

60) $3.65 \times 1.4 =$

61) $24.82 \div 0.4 =$

62) $12.4 \times 4.20 =$

Effortless Math Education

Chapter 2: Answers

1)	<	22)	16	43)	26.48
2)	>	23)	13	44)	48.69
3)	<	24)	17	45)	34.18
4)	<	25)	68	46)	62.58
5)	<	26)	43	47)	0.66
6)	>	27)	56	48)	8
7)	>	28)	14	49)	11.34
8)	<	29)	79	50)	24
9)	<	30)	98	51)	1.23
10)	<	31)	48.3	52)	43
11)	=	32)	34.1	53)	7.92
12)	=	33)	57.9	54)	9.2
13)	=	34)	11.5	55)	17.64
14)	<	35)	42.2	56)	7.2
15)	6	36)	41.67	57)	28.52
16)	6	37)	61.89	58)	22.875
17)	12	38)	14.04	59)	9.932
18)	9	39)	67.91	60)	5.11
19)	8	40)	124.79	61)	62.05
20)	22	41)	6.77	62)	52.08
21)	7	42)	121.48		

Effortless
Math
Education

CHAPTER

3 Integers and Order of Operations

Math topics that you'll learn in this chapter:

- ☑ Adding and Subtracting Integers
- ☑ Multiplying and Dividing Integers
- ☑ Order of Operations
- ☑ Integers and Absolute Value

21

Adding and Subtracting Integers

- Integers include zero, counting numbers, and the negative of the counting numbers. $\{\dots, -3, -2, -1, 0, 1, 2, 3, \dots\}$

- Add a positive integer by moving to the right on the number line. (you will get a bigger number)

- Add a negative integer by moving to the left on the number line. (you will get a smaller number)

- Subtract an integer by adding its opposite.

Examples:

Example 1. Solve. $(-2) - (-8) =$

Solution: Keep the first number and convert the sign of the second number to its opposite. (change subtraction into addition. Then: $(-2) + 8 = 6$

Example 2. Solve. $4 + (5 - 10) =$

Solution: First, subtract the numbers in brackets, $5 - 10 = -5$.
Then: $4 + (-5) = \rightarrow$ change addition into subtraction: $4 - 5 = -1$

Example 3. Solve. $(9 - 14) + 15 =$

Solution: First, subtract the numbers in brackets, $9 - 14 = -5$
Then: $-5 + 15 = \rightarrow -5 + 15 = 10$

Example 4. Solve. $12 + (-3 - 10) =$

Solution: First, subtract the numbers in brackets, $-3 - 10 = -13$
Then: $12 + (-13) = \rightarrow$ change addition into subtraction: $12 - 13 = -1$

Multiplying and Dividing Integers

Use the following rules for multiplying and dividing integers:

- (negative) × (negative) = positive

- (negative) ÷ (negative) = positive

- (negative) × (positive) = negative

- (negative) ÷ (positive) = negative

- (positive) × (positive) = positive

- (positive) ÷ (negative) = negative

Examples:

Example 1. Solve. $3 \times (-4) =$

Solution: Use this rule: (positive) × (negative) = negative.
Then: $(3) \times (-4) = -12$

Example 2. Solve. $(-3) + (-24 \div 3) =$

Solution: First, divide -24 by 3, the numbers in brackets, use this rule:
(negative) ÷ (positive) = negative. Then: $-24 \div 3 = -8$
$(-3) + (-24 \div 3) = (-3) + (-8) = -3 - 8 = -11$

Example 3. Solve. $(12 - 15) \times (-2) =$

Solution: First, subtract the numbers in brackets,
$12 - 15 = -3 \rightarrow (-3) \times (-2) =$
Now use this rule: (negative) × (negative) = positive $\rightarrow (-3) \times (-2) = 6$

Example 4. Solve. $(12 - 8) \div (-4) =$

Solution: First, subtract the numbers in brackets,
$12 - 8 = 4 \rightarrow (4) \div (-4) =$
Now use this rule: (positive) ÷ (negative) = negative $\rightarrow (4) \div (-4) =$
-1

bit.ly/3pjQW98
Find more at

Order of Operations

- In Mathematics, "operations" are addition, subtraction, multiplication, division, exponentiation (written as b^n), and grouping.

- When there is more than one math operation in an expression, use PEMDAS: (to memorize this rule, remember the phrase "Please Excuse My Dear Aunt Sally".)

  ❖ Parentheses

  ❖ Exponents

  ❖ Multiplication and Division (from left to right)

  ❖ Addition and Subtraction (from left to right)

Examples:

Example 1. Calculate. $(2 + 6) \div (2^2 \div 4) =$

Solution: First, simplify inside parentheses:
$(8) \div (4 \div 4) = (8) \div (1)$, Then: $(8) \div (1) = 8$

Example 2. Solve. $(6 \times 5) - (14 - 5) =$

Solution: First, calculate within parentheses: $(6 \times 5) - (14 - 5) = (30) - (9)$, Then: $(30) - (9) = 21$

Example 3. Calculate. $-4[(3 \times 6) \div (3^2 \times 2)] =$

Solution: First, calculate within parentheses:
$-4[(18) \div (9 \times 2)] = -4[(18) \div (18)] = -4[1]$
multiply -4 and 1. Then: $-4[1] = -4$

Example 4. Solve. $(28 \div 7) + (-19 + 3) =$

Solution: First, calculate within parentheses:
$(28 \div 7) + (-19 + 3) = (4) + (-16)$ Then: $(4) - (16) = -12$

Integers and Absolute Value

- The absolute value of a number is its distance from zero, in either direction, on the number line. For example, the distance of 9 and -9 from zero on number line is 9.

- The absolute value of an integer is the numerical value without its sign. (negative or positive)

- The vertical bar is used for absolute value as in $|x|$.

- The absolute value of a number is never negative; because it only shows, "how far the number is from zero".

Examples:

Example 1. Calculate. $|14 - 2| \times 5 =$

Solution: First, solve $|14 - 2|$, $\rightarrow |14 - 2| = |12|$, the absolute value of 12 is 12, $|12| = 12$ Then: $12 \times 5 = 60$

Example 2. Solve. $\frac{|-24|}{4} \times |5 - 7| =$

Solution: First, find $|-24|$, $\rightarrow$ the absolute value of -24 is 24,
Then: $|-24| = 24$, $\frac{24}{4} \times |5 - 7| =$

Now, calculate $|5 - 7|$, $\rightarrow |5 - 7| = |-2|$, the absolute value of -2 is 2. $|-2| = 2$
then: $\frac{24}{4} \times 2 = 6 \times 2 = 12$

Example 3. Solve. $|8 - 2| \times \frac{|-4 \times 7|}{2} =$

Solution: First, calculate $|8 - 2|$, $\rightarrow |8 - 2| = |6|$, the absolute value of 6 is 6, $|6| = 6$. Then: $6 \times \frac{|-4 \times 7|}{2}$

Now calculate $|-4 \times 7|$, $\rightarrow |-4 \times 7| = |-28|$, the absolute value of -28 is 28, $|-28| = 28$ Then: $6 \times \frac{28}{2} = 6 \times 14 = 84$

Chapter 3: Practices

✍ Find each sum or difference.

1) $-9 + 16 =$

2) $-18 - 6 =$

3) $-24 + 10 =$

4) $30 + (-5) =$

5) $15 + (-3) =$

6) $(-13) + (-4) =$

7) $25 + (3 - 10) =$

8) $12 - (-6 + 9) =$

9) $5 - (-2 + 7) =$

10) $(-11) + (-5 + 6) =$

11) $(-3) + (9 - 16) =$

12) $(-8) - (13 + 4) =$

13) $(-7 + 9) - 39 =$

14) $(-30 + 6) - 14 =$

15) $(-5 + 9) + (-3 + 7) =$

16) $(8 - 19) - (-4 + 12) =$

17) $(-9 + 2) - (6 - 7) =$

18) $(-12 - 5) - (-4 - 14) =$

✍ Solve.

19) $3 \times (-6) =$

20) $(-32) \div 4 =$

21) $(-5) \times 4 =$

22) $(25) \div (-5) =$

23) $(-72) \div 8 =$

24) $(-2) \times (-6) \times 5 =$

25) $(-2) \times 3 \times (-7) =$

26) $(-1) \times (-3) \times (-5) =$

27) $(-2) \times (-3) \times (-6) =$

28) $(-12 + 3) \times (-5) =$

29) $(-3 + 4) \times (-11) =$

30) $(-9) \times (6 - 5) =$

31) $(-3 - 7) \times (-6) =$

32) $(-7 + 3) \times (-9 + 6) =$

33) $(-15) \div (-17 + 12) =$

34) $(-3 - 2) \times (-9 + 7) =$

35) $(-15 + 31) \div (-2) =$

36) $(-64) \div (-16 + 8) =$

Effortless Math Education

✏ Evaluate each expression.

37) $3 + (2 \times 5) =$

38) $(5 \times 4) - 7 =$

39) $(-9 \times 2) + 6 =$

40) $(7 \times 3) - (-5) =$

41) $(-8) + (2 \times 7) =$

42) $(9 - 6) + (3 \times 4) =$

43) $(-19 + 5) + (6 \times 2) =$

44) $(32 \div 4) + (1 - 13) =$

45) $(-36 \div 6) - (12 + 3) =$

46) $(-16 + 5) - (54 \div 9) =$

47) $(-20 + 4) - (35 \div 5) =$

48) $(42 \div 7) + (2 \times 3) =$

49) $(28 \div 4) + (2 \times 6) =$

50) $2[(3 \times 3) - (4 \times 5)] =$

51) $3[(2 \times 8) + (4 \times 3)] =$

52) $2[(9 \times 3) - (6 \times 4)] =$

53) $4[(4 \times 8) \div (4 \times 4)] =$

54) $-5[(10 \times 8) \div (5 \times 8)] =$

✏ Find the answers.

55) $|-5| + |7 - 10| =$

56) $|-4 + 6| + |-2| =$

57) $|-9| + |1 - 9| =$

58) $|-7| - |8 - 12| =$

59) $|9 - 11| + |8 - 15| =$

60) $|-7 + 10| - |-8 + 3| =$

61) $|-12 + 6| - |3 - 9| =$

62) $5 + |2 - 6| + |3 - 4| =$

63) $-4 + |2 - 6| + |1 - 9| =$

64) $|-6| \times |-7| + |2 - 8| =$

65) $|-12| \times |-3| + |4 - 28| =$

66) $|4 \times (-2)| \times |-9| =$

67) $|-3 \times 2| \times |-5| =$

68) $|3 - 12| - |-3 \times 7| =$

69) $|-9| + |-7 \times 5| =$

70) $|-11| + |-6 \times 4| =$

71) $|-4 \times 2 + 6| \times |-2 \times 8| =$

72) $|-1 \times 5 + 2| \times |-4| =$

Effortless Math Education

Chapter 3: Answers

1)	7	25)	42	49)	19
2)	−24	26)	−15	50)	−22
3)	−14	27)	−36	51)	84
4)	25	28)	45	52)	6
5)	12	29)	−11	53)	8
6)	−17	30)	−9	54)	−10
7)	18	31)	60	55)	8
8)	9	32)	12	56)	4
9)	0	33)	3	57)	17
10)	−10	34)	10	58)	3
11)	−10	35)	−8	59)	9
12)	−25	36)	8	60)	−2
13)	−37	37)	13	61)	0
14)	−38	38)	13	62)	10
15)	8	39)	−12	63)	8
16)	−19	40)	26	64)	48
17)	−6	41)	6	65)	60
18)	1	42)	15	66)	72
19)	−18	43)	−2	67)	30
20)	−8	44)	−4	68)	−12
21)	−20	45)	−21	69)	44
22)	−5	46)	−17	70)	35
23)	−9	47)	−23	71)	32
24)	60	48)	12	72)	12

Effortless Math Education

4 Ratios and Proportions

Math topics that you'll learn in this chapter:

☑ Simplifying Ratios

☑ Proportional Ratios

☑ Similarity and Ratios

29

Simplifying Ratios

- Ratios are used to make comparisons between two numbers.

- Ratios can be written as a fraction, using the word "to", or with a colon. Example: $\frac{3}{4}$ or "3 to 4" or 3:4

- You can calculate equivalent ratios by multiplying or dividing both sides of the ratio by the same number.

Examples:

Example 1. Simplify. $8:2 =$

Solution: Both numbers 8 and 2 are divisible by 2 , $\Rightarrow 8 \div 2 = 4$, $4 \div 2 = 2$, Then: $8:2 = 4:1$

Example 2. Simplify. $\frac{9}{33} =$

Solution: Both numbers 9 and 33 are divisible by 3, $\Rightarrow$ $33 \div 3 = 11$, $9 \div 3 = 3$, Then: $\frac{9}{33} = \frac{3}{11}$

Example 3. There are 24 students in a class and 10 are girls. Write the ratio of girls to boys.

Solution: Subtract 10 from 24 to find the number of boys in the class.
$24 - 10 = 14$. There are 14 boys in the class. So, the ratio of girls to boys is $10:14$.
Now, simplify this ratio. Both 14 and 10 are divisible by 2.
Then: $14 \div 2 = 7$, and $10 \div 2 = 5$. In the simplest form, this ratio is $5:7$

Example 4. A recipe calls for butter and sugar in the ratio $3:4$. If you're using 9 cups of butter, how many cups of sugar should you use?

Solution: Since you use 9 cups of butter, or 3 times as much, you need to multiply the amount of sugar by 3. Then: $4 \times 3 = 12$. So, you need to use 12 cups of sugar. You can solve this using equivalent fractions:
$\frac{3}{4} = \frac{9}{12}$

Proportional Ratios

- Two ratios are proportional if they represent the same relationship.

- A proportion means that two ratios are equal. It can be written in two ways:

$$\frac{a}{b} = \frac{c}{d} \qquad a : b = c : d$$

- The proportion $\frac{a}{b} = \frac{c}{d}$ can be written as: $a \times d = c \times b$

Examples:

Example 1. Solve this proportion for x. $\frac{2}{5} = \frac{6}{x}$

Solution: Use cross multiplication: $\frac{2}{5} = \frac{6}{x} \Rightarrow 2 \times x = 6 \times 5 \Rightarrow 2x = 30$

Divide both sides by 2 to find x: $x = \frac{30}{2} \Rightarrow x = 15$

Example 2. If a box contains red and blue balls in ratio of $3 : 5$ red to blue, how many red balls are there if 45 blue balls are in the box?

Solution: Write a proportion and solve. $\frac{3}{5} = \frac{x}{45}$

Use cross multiplication: $3 \times 45 = 5 \times x \Rightarrow 135 = 5x$

Divide to find x: $x = \frac{135}{5} \Rightarrow x = 27$. There are 27 red balls in the box.

Example 3. Solve this proportion for x. $\frac{4}{9} = \frac{16}{x}$

Solution: Use cross multiplication: $\frac{4}{9} = \frac{16}{x} \Rightarrow 4 \times x = 9 \times 16 \Rightarrow 4x = 144$

Divide to find x: $x = \frac{144}{4} \Rightarrow x = 36$

Example 4. Solve this proportion for x. $\frac{5}{7} = \frac{20}{x}$

Solution: Use cross multiplication: $\frac{5}{7} = \frac{20}{x} \Rightarrow 5 \times x = 7 \times 20 \Rightarrow 5x = 140$

Divide to find x: $x = \frac{140}{5} \Rightarrow x = 28$

bit.ly/37GHQxp

Find more at

Similarity and Ratios

- Two figures are similar if they have the same shape.

- Two or more figures are similar if the corresponding angles are equal, and the corresponding sides are in proportion.

Examples:

Example 1. The following triangles are similar. What is the value of the unknown side?

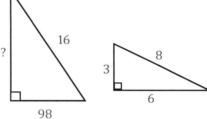

Solution: Find the corresponding sides and write a proportion.
$\frac{8}{16} = \frac{6}{x}$. Now, use the cross product to solve for x:
$\frac{8}{16} = \frac{6}{x} \rightarrow 8 \times x = 16 \times 6 \rightarrow 8x = 96$. Divide both sides by 8. Then: $8x = 96 \rightarrow x = \frac{96}{8} \rightarrow x = 12$

The missing side is 12.

Example 2. Two rectangles are similar. The first is 5 feet wide and 15 feet long. The second is 10 feet wide. What is the length of the second rectangle?

Solution: Let's put x for the length of the second rectangle. Since two rectangles are similar, their corresponding sides are in proportion. Write a proportion and solve for the missing number.
$\frac{5}{10} = \frac{15}{x} \rightarrow 5x = 10 \times 15 \rightarrow 5x = 150 \rightarrow x = \frac{150}{5} = 30$
The length of the second rectangle is 30 feet.

Chapter 4: Practices

✍ Reduce each ratio.

1) $2:18 =$ ___ : ___

2) $5:35 =$ ___ : ___

3) $8:72 =$ ___ : ___

4) $24:36 =$ ___ : ___

5) $25:40 =$ ___ : ___

6) $40:72 =$ ___ : ___

7) $28:63 =$ ___ : ___

8) $18:81 =$ ___ : ___

9) $13:52 =$ ___ : ___

10) $56:72 =$ ___ : ___

11) $42:63 =$ ___ : ___

12) $32:96 =$ ___ : ___

✍ Solve.

13) Bob has 16 red cards and 20 green cards. What is the ratio of Bob's red cards to his green cards? _____

14) In a party, 34 soft drinks are required for every 20 guests. If there are 260 guests, how many soft drinks are required? _____

15) Sara has 56 blue pens and 28 black pens. What is the ratio of Sara's black pens to her blue pens? _____

16) In Jack's class, 48 of the students are tall and 20 are short. In Michael's class 28 students are tall and 12 students are short. Which class has a higher ratio of tall to short students? _____

17) The price of 6 apples at the Quick Market is $1.52. The price of 5 of the same apples at Walmart is $1.32. Which place is the better buy? _____

18) The bakers at a Bakery can make 180 bagels in 6 hours. How many bagels can they bake in 16 hours? What is that rate per hour? _____

19) You can buy 6 cans of green beans at a supermarket for $3.48. How much does it cost to buy 38 cans of green beans? _____

Effortless Math Education

✍ Solve each proportion.

20) $\frac{3}{2} = \frac{9}{x} \Rightarrow x =$ _____

21) $\frac{7}{2} = \frac{x}{4} \Rightarrow x =$ _____

22) $\frac{1}{3} = \frac{2}{x} \Rightarrow x =$ _____

23) $\frac{1}{4} = \frac{5}{x} \Rightarrow x =$ _____

24) $\frac{9}{6} = \frac{x}{2} \Rightarrow x =$ _____

25) $\frac{3}{6} = \frac{5}{x} \Rightarrow x =$ _____

26) $\frac{7}{x} = \frac{2}{6} \Rightarrow x =$ _____

27) $\frac{2}{x} = \frac{4}{10} \Rightarrow x =$ _____

28) $\frac{3}{2} = \frac{x}{8} \Rightarrow x =$ _____

29) $\frac{x}{6} = \frac{5}{3} \Rightarrow x =$ _____

30) $\frac{3}{9} = \frac{5}{x} \Rightarrow x =$ _____

31) $\frac{4}{18} = \frac{2}{x} \Rightarrow x =$ _____

32) $\frac{6}{16} = \frac{3}{x} \Rightarrow x =$ _____

33) $\frac{2}{5} = \frac{x}{20} \Rightarrow x =$ _____

34) $\frac{28}{8} = \frac{x}{2} \Rightarrow x =$ _____

35) $\frac{3}{5} = \frac{x}{15} \Rightarrow x =$ _____

36) $\frac{2}{7} = \frac{x}{14} \Rightarrow x =$ _____

37) $\frac{x}{18} = \frac{3}{2} \Rightarrow x =$ _____

38) $\frac{x}{24} = \frac{2}{6} \Rightarrow x =$ _____

39) $\frac{5}{x} = \frac{4}{20} \Rightarrow x =$ _____

40) $\frac{10}{x} = \frac{20}{80} \Rightarrow x =$ _____

41) $\frac{90}{6} = \frac{x}{2} \Rightarrow x =$ _____

✍ Solve each problem.

42) Two rectangles are similar. The first is 8 *feet* wide and 32 *feet* long. The second is 12 *feet* wide. What is the length of the second rectangle?

_____

43) Two rectangles are similar. One is 4.6 *meters* by 7 *meters*. The longer side of the second rectangle is 28 *meters*. What is the other side of the second rectangle? _____

Effortless
Math
Education

Effortless Math Education

Chapter 4: Answers

1) $1:9$

2) $1:7$

3) $1:9$

4) $2:3$

5) $5:8$

6) $5:9$

7) $4:9$

8) $2:9$

9) $1:4$

10) $7:9$

11) $2:3$

12) $1:3$

13) $4:5$

14) 442

15) $1:2$

16) *Jack's class*: $\frac{48}{20} = \frac{12}{5}$ *Michael's class*: $\frac{28}{12} = \frac{7}{3}$ Jack's class has a higher ratio of tall to short student: $\frac{12}{5} > \frac{7}{3}$

17) Quick market

18) 480, 30 bagels per hour

19) $22.04

20) 6

21) 14

22) 6

23) 20

24) 3

25) 10

26) 21

27) 5

28) 12

29) 10

30) 15

31) 9

32) 8

33) 8

34) 7

35) 9

36) 4

37) 27

38) 8

39) 25

40) 40

41) 30

42) 48 *meters*

43) 18.4 *meters*

5 Percentage

Math topics that you'll learn in this chapter:

- ☑ Percent Problems
- ☑ Percent of Increase and Decrease
- ☑ Discount, Tax and Tip
- ☑ Simple Interest

37

Percent Problems

- Percent is a ratio of a number and 100. It always has the same denominator, 100. The percent symbol is "%".

- Percent means "per 100". So, 20% is 20/100.

- In each percent problem, we are looking for the base, or part or the percent.

- Use these equations to find each missing section in a percent problem:

   ❖ Base = Part ÷ Percent

   ❖ Part = Percent × Base

   ❖ Percent = Part ÷ Base

Examples:

Example 1. What is 20% of 40?

Solution: In this problem, we have percent (20%) and base (40) and we are looking for the "part". Use this formula: *part = percent × base*.

Then: $part = 20\% \times 40 = \frac{20}{100} \times 40 = 0.20 \times 40 = 8$. The answer: 20% of 40 is 8.

Example 2. 25 is what percent of 500?

Solution: In this problem, we are looking for the percent. Use this equation: $Percent = Part \div Base \rightarrow Percent = 25 \div 500 = 0.05 = 5\%$.
Then: 25 is 5 percent of 500.

Percent of Increase and Decrease

- Percent of change (increase or decrease) is a mathematical concept that represents the degree of change over time.

- To find the percentage of increase or decrease:

  1. New Number – Original Number
  2. The result ÷ Original Number × 100

- Or use this formula: Percent of change $= \frac{new\ number - original\ number}{original\ number} \times 100$

- Note: If your answer is a negative number, then this is a percentage decrease. If it is positive, then this is a percentage increase.

Examples:

Example 1. The price of a shirt increases from \$30 to \$40. What is the percentage increase?

Solution: First, find the difference: $40 - 30 = 10$

Then: $10 \div 30 \times 100 = \frac{10}{30} \times 100 = 33.33$. The percentage increase is 33.33. It means that the price of the shirt increased by 33.33%.

Example 2. The price of a table increased from \$20 to \$50. What is the percent of increase?

Solution: Use percentage formula:

$$Percent\ of\ change = \frac{new\ number - original\ number}{original\ number} \times 100 =$$

$\frac{50-20}{20} \times 100 = \frac{30}{20} \times 100 = 1.5 \times 100 = 150$. The percentage increase is 150. It means that the price of the table increased by 150%.

bit.ly/3pgPQes

Find more at

Discount, Tax and Tip

- To find the discount: Multiply the regular price by the rate of discount

- To find the selling price: Original price – discount

- To find tax: Multiply the tax rate to the taxable amount (income, property value, etc.)

- To find the tip, multiply the rate to the selling price.

Examples:

Example 1. With an 20% discount, Ella saved $50 on a dress. What was the original price of the dress?

Solution: let x be the original price of the dress. Then: 20 % *of* $x = 50$. Write an equation and solve for x: $0.20 \times x = 50 \rightarrow x = \frac{50}{0.20} = 250$. The original price of the dress was $250.

Example 2. Sophia purchased a new computer for a price of $820 at the Apple Store. What is the total amount her credit card is charged if the sales tax is 5%?

Solution: The taxable amount is $820, and the tax rate is 5%. Then: $Tax = 0.05 \times 820 = 41$

Final price = Selling price + Tax → final price = $820 + $41 = $861

Example 3. Nicole and her friends went out to eat at a restaurant. If their bill was $60.00 and they gave their server a 15% tip, how much did they pay altogether?

Solution: First, find the tip. To find the tip, multiply the rate to the bill amount. $Tip = 60 \times 0.15 = 9$. The final price is: $60 + $9 = $69

Simple Interest

- Simple Interest: The charge for borrowing money or the return for lending it.

- Simple interest is calculated on the initial amount (principal).

- To solve a simple interest problem, use this formula:

  Interest = principal × rate × time $(I = p \times r \times t = prt)$

Examples:

Example 1. Find simple interest for $200 investment at 5% for 3 years.

Solution: Use Interest formula:
$I = prt$ $(P = \$200$, r $= 5\% = \frac{5}{100} = 0.05$ and $t = 3)$
Then: $I = 200 \times 0.05 \times 3 = \$30$

Example 2. Find simple interest for $1,200 at 8% for 6 years.

Solution: Use Interest formula:
$I = prt$ $(P = \$1,200$, r $= 8\% = \frac{8}{100} = 0.08$ and $t = 6)$
Then: $I = 1,200 \times 0.08 \times 6 = \$576$

Example 3. Andy received a student loan to pay for his educational expenses this year. What is the interest on the loan if he borrowed $4,500 at 6% for 5 years?

Solution: Use Interest formula: $I = prt$. $P = \$4,500$, r $= 6\% = 0.06$ and $t = 5$
Then: $I = 4,500 \times 0.06 \times 5 = \$1,350$

Example 4. Bob is starting his own small business. He borrowed $20,000 from the bank at a 8% rate for 6 months. Find the interest Bob will pay on this loan.

Solution: Use Interest formula:
$I = prt$. $P = \$20,000$, r $= 8\% = 0.08$ and $t = 0.5$ (6 months is half year). Then: $I = 20,000 \times 0.08 \times 0.5 = \$800$

bit.ly/3nJli3D

Find more at

Chapter 5: Practices

✎ Solve each problem.

1) What is 15% of 60? ____

2) What is 55% of 800? ____

3) What is 22% of 120? ____

4) What is 18% of 40? ____

5) 90 is what percent of 200? ____%

6) 30 is what percent of 150? ____%

7) 14 is what percent of 250? ____%

8) 60 is what percent of 300? ____%

9) 30 is 120 percent of what number? ____

10) 120 is 20 percent of what number? ____

11) 15 is 5 percent of what number? ____

12) 22 is 20% of what number? ____

✎ Solve each problem.

13) Bob got a raise, and his hourly wage increased from $15 to $21. What is the percent increase? _____ %

14) The price of a pair of shoes increases from $32 to $36. What is the percent increase? ___ %

15) At a Coffee Shop, the price of a cup of coffee increased from $1.35 to $1.62. What is the percent increase in the cost of the coffee? _____ %

16) A $45 shirt now selling for $36 is discounted by what percent? _____ %

17) Joe scored 30 out of 35 marks in Algebra, 20 out of 30 marks in science and 58 out of 70 marks in mathematics. In which subject his percentage of marks is best? _____

18) Emma purchased a computer for $420. The computer is regularly priced at $480. What was the percent discount Emma received on the computer? _____

19) A chemical solution contains 15% alcohol. If there is 54 ml of alcohol, what is the volume of the solution? _____

Effortless
Math
Education

🪶 Find the selling price of each item.

20) Original price of a computer: $600

Tax: 8%, Selling price: $_____

21) Original price of a laptop: $450

Tax: 10%, Selling price: $_____

22) Nicolas hired a moving company. The company charged $500 for its services, and Nicolas gives the movers a 14% tip. How much does Nicolas tip the movers? $_____

23) Mason has lunch at a restaurant and the cost of his meal is $40. Mason wants to leave a 20% tip. What is Mason's total bill, including tip? $_____

🪶 Determine the simple interest for the following loans.

24) $1,000 at 5% for 4 $years.$ $__

25) $400 at 3% for 5 $years.$ $__

26) $240 at 4% for 3 $years.$ $__

27) $500 at 4.5% for 6 years. $__

🪶 Solve.

28) A new car, valued at $20,000, depreciates at 8% per year. What is the value of the car one year after purchase? $_____

29) Sara puts $7,000 into an investment yielding 3% annual simple interest; she left the money in for five years. How much interest does Sara get at the end of those five years? $_____

Effortless Math Education

Chapter 5: Answers

1) 9

2) 440

3) 26.4

4) 7.2

5) 45%

6) 20%

7) 5.6%

8) 20%

9) 25

10) 600

11) 300

12) 110

13) 40%

14) 12.5%

15) 20%

16) 20%

17) Algebra

18) 12.5%

19) 360 ml

20) $648.00

21) $495.00

22) $70.00

23) $48.00

24) $200.00

25) $60.00

26) $28.80

27) $135.00

28) $18.400

29) $1,050

CHAPTER

6 Exponents and Variables

Math topics that you'll learn in this chapter:

- ☑ Multiplication Property of Exponents
- ☑ Division Property of Exponents
- ☑ Powers of Products and Quotients
- ☑ Zero and Negative Exponents
- ☑ Negative Exponents and Negative Bases
- ☑ Scientific Notation
- ☑ Radicals

Multiplication Property of Exponents

- Exponents are shorthand for repeated multiplication of the same number by itself. For example, instead of 2×2, we can write 2^2. For $3 \times 3 \times 3 \times 3$, we can write 3^4

- In algebra, a variable is a letter used to stand for a number. The most common letters are: $x, y, z, a, b, c, m,$ and n.

- Exponent's rules: $x^a \times x^b = x^{a+b}$, $\dfrac{x^a}{x^b} = x^{a-b}$

$$(x^a)^b = x^{a \times b} \qquad\qquad (xy)^a = x^a \times y^a \qquad\qquad \left(\dfrac{a}{b}\right)^c = \dfrac{a^c}{b^c}$$

Examples:

Example 1. Multiply. $2x^2 \times 3x^4$

Solution: Use Exponent's rules: $x^a \times x^b = x^{a+b} \rightarrow x^2 \times x^4 = x^{2+4} = x^6$
Then: $2x^2 \times 3x^4 = 6x^6$

Example 2. Simplify. $(x^4y^2)^2$

Solution: Use Exponent's rules: $(x^a)^b = x^{a \times b}$.
Then: $(x^4y^2)^2 = x^{4\times2}y^{2\times2} = x^8y^4$

Example 3. Multiply. $5x^8 \times 6x^5$

Solution: Use Exponent's rules: $x^a \times x^b = x^{a+b} \rightarrow x^8 \times x^5 = x^{8+5} = x^{13}$
Then: $5x^8 \times 6x^5 = 30x^{13}$

Example 4. Simplify. $(x^4y^7)^3$

Solution: Use Exponent's rules: $(x^a)^b = x^{a \times b}$.
Then: $(x^4y^7)^3 = x^{4\times3}y^{7\times3} = x^{12}y^{21}$

Division Property of Exponents

- Exponents are shorthand for repeated multiplication of the same number by itself. For example, instead of 3×3, we can write 3^2. For $2 \times 2 \times 2$, we can write 2^3

- For division of exponents use following formulas:

$$\frac{x^a}{x^b} = x^{a-b} \ , \ x \neq 0, \ \frac{x^a}{x^b} = \frac{1}{x^{b-a}} \ , \ x \neq 0, \qquad \frac{1}{x^b} = x^{-b}$$

Examples:

Example 1. Simplify. $\frac{16x^3y}{2xy^2} =$

Solution: First, cancel the common factor: $2 \rightarrow \frac{16x^3y}{2xy^2} = \frac{8x^3y}{xy^2}$

Use Exponent's rules: $\frac{x^a}{x^b} = x^{a-b} \ \rightarrow \frac{x^3}{x} = x^{3-1} = x^2$ and $\frac{y}{y^2} = \frac{1}{y^{2-1}} = \frac{1}{y}$

Then: $\frac{16x^3y}{2xy^2} = \frac{8x^2}{y}$

Example 2. Simplify. $\frac{24x^8}{3x^6} =$

Solution: Use Exponent's rules: $\frac{x^a}{x^b} = x^{b-a} \ \rightarrow \frac{x^8}{x^6} = x^{8-6} = x^2$

Then: $\frac{24x^8}{3x^6} = 8x^2$

Example 3. Simplify. $\frac{7x^4y^2}{28x^3\text{y}} =$

Solution: First, cancel the common factor: $7 \rightarrow \frac{x^4y^2}{4x^3\text{y}}$

Use Exponent's rules: $\frac{x^a}{x^b} = x^{a-b} \ \rightarrow \frac{x^4}{x^3} = x^{4-3} = x$ and $\frac{y^2}{\text{y}} = y$

Then: $\frac{7x^4y^2}{28x^3\text{y}} = \frac{xy}{4}$

bit.ly/37JAclZ

Find more at

Powers of Products and Quotients

- Exponents are shorthand for repeated multiplication of the same number by itself. For example, instead of $2 \times 2 \times 2$, we can write 2^3. For $3 \times 3 \times 3 \times 3$, we can write 3^4

- For any nonzero numbers a and b and any integer x, $(ab)^x = a^x \times b^x$ and $\left(\frac{a}{b}\right)^c = \frac{a^c}{b^c}$

Examples:

Example 1. Simplify. $(3x^3y^2)^2$

Solution: Use Exponent's rules: $(x^a)^b = x^{a \times b}$
$(3x^3y^2)^2 = (3)^2(x^3)^2(y^2)^2 = 9x^{3 \times 2}y^{2 \times 2} = 9x^6y^4$

Example 2. Simplify. $\left(\frac{2x^3}{3x^2}\right)^2$

Solution: First, cancel the common factor: $x \rightarrow \left(\frac{2x^3}{3x^2}\right) = \left(\frac{2x}{3}\right)^2$
Use Exponent's rules: $\left(\frac{a}{b}\right)^c = \frac{a^c}{b^c}$, Then: $\left(\frac{2x}{3}\right)^2 = \frac{(2x)^2}{(3)^2} = \frac{4x^2}{9}$

Example 3. Simplify. $\left(-4x^3y^5\right)^2$

Solution: Use Exponent's rules: $(x^a)^b = x^{a \times b}$
$$\left(-4x^3y^5\right)^2 = (-4)^2(x^3)^2\left(y^5\right)^2 = 16x^{3 \times 2}y^{5 \times 2} = 16x^6y^{10}$$

Example 4. Simplify. $\left(\frac{5x}{4x^2}\right)^2$

Solution: First, cancel the common factor: $x \rightarrow \left(\frac{5x}{4x^2}\right)^2 = \left(\frac{5}{4x}\right)^2$
Use Exponent's rules: $\left(\frac{a}{b}\right)^c = \frac{a^c}{b^c}$, Then: $\left(\frac{5}{4x}\right)^2 = \frac{5^2}{(4x)^2} = \frac{25}{16x^2}$

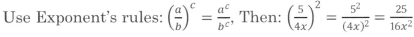

Zero and Negative Exponents

- Zero-Exponent Rule: $a^0 = 1$, this means that anything raised to the zero power is 1. For example: $(5xy)^0 = 1$

- A negative exponent simply means that the base is on the wrong side of the fraction line, so you need to flip the base to the other side. For instance, "x^{-2}" (pronounced as "ecks to the minus two") just means "x^2" but underneath, as in $\frac{1}{x^2}$.

Examples:

Example 1. Evaluate. $\left(\frac{4}{5}\right)^{-2} =$

Solution: Use negative exponent's rule: $\left(\frac{x^a}{x^b}\right)^{-2} = \left(\frac{x^b}{x^a}\right)^{2} \rightarrow \left(\frac{4}{5}\right)^{-2} = \left(\frac{5}{4}\right)^{2} =$
Then: $\left(\frac{5}{4}\right)^{2} = \frac{5^2}{4^2} = \frac{25}{16}$

Example 2. Evaluate. $\left(\frac{3}{2}\right)^{-3} =$

Solution: Use negative exponent's rule: $\left(\frac{x^a}{x^b}\right)^{-3} = \left(\frac{x^b}{x^a}\right)^{3} \rightarrow \left(\frac{3}{2}\right)^{-3} = \left(\frac{2}{3}\right)^{3} =$
Then: $\left(\frac{2}{3}\right)^{3} = \frac{2^3}{3^3} = \frac{8}{27}$

Example 3. Evaluate. $\left(\frac{a}{b}\right)^{0} =$

Solution: Use zero-exponent Rule: $a^0 = 1$
Then: $\left(\frac{a}{b}\right)^{0} = 1$

Example 4. Evaluate. $\left(\frac{4}{7}\right)^{-1} =$

Solution: Use negative exponent's rule: $\left(\frac{x^a}{x^b}\right)^{-1} = \left(\frac{x^b}{x^a}\right)^{1} \rightarrow \left(\frac{4}{7}\right)^{-1} = \left(\frac{7}{4}\right)^{1} = \frac{7}{4}$

Find more at bit.ly/3rnkh4v

Negative Exponents and Negative Bases

- A negative exponent is the reciprocal of that number with a positive exponent.
$(3)^{-2} = \frac{1}{3^2}$

- To simplify a negative exponent, make the power positive!

- The parenthesis is important! -5^{-2} is not the same as $(-5)^{-2}$

$$-5^{-2} = -\frac{1}{5^2} \text{ and } (-5)^{-2} = +\frac{1}{5^2}$$

Examples:

Example 1. Simplify. $\left(\frac{2a}{3c}\right)^{-2} =$

Solution: Use negative exponent's rule: $\left(\frac{x^a}{x^b}\right)^{-2} = \left(\frac{x^b}{x^a}\right)^2 \rightarrow \left(\frac{2a}{3c}\right)^{-2} = \left(\frac{3c}{2a}\right)^2$

Now use exponent's rule: $\left(\frac{a}{b}\right)^c = \frac{a^c}{b^c} \rightarrow = \left(\frac{3c}{2a}\right)^2 = \frac{3^2c^2}{2^2a^2}$

Then: $\frac{3^2c^2}{2^2a^2} = \frac{9c^2}{4a^2}$

Example 2. Simplify. $\left(\frac{x}{4y}\right)^{-3} =$

Solution: Use negative exponent's rule: $\left(\frac{x^a}{x^b}\right)^{-3} = \left(\frac{x^b}{x^a}\right)^3 \rightarrow \left(\frac{x}{4y}\right)^{-3} = \left(\frac{4y}{x}\right)^3$

Now use exponent's rule: $\left(\frac{a}{b}\right)^c = \frac{a^c}{b^c} \rightarrow \left(\frac{4y}{x}\right)^3 = \frac{4^3y^3}{x^3} = \frac{64y^3}{x^3}$

Example 3. Simplify. $\left(\frac{5a}{2c}\right)^{-2} =$

Solution: Use negative exponent's rule: $\left(\frac{x^a}{x^b}\right)^{-2} = \left(\frac{x^b}{x^a}\right)^2 \rightarrow \left(\frac{5a}{2c}\right)^{-2} = \left(\frac{2c}{5a}\right)^2$

Now use exponent's rule: $\left(\frac{a}{b}\right)^c = \frac{a^c}{b^c} \rightarrow = \left(\frac{2c}{5a}\right)^2 = \frac{2^2c^2}{5^2a^2}$

Then: $\frac{2^2c^2}{5^2a^2} = \frac{4c^2}{25a^2}$

Scientific Notation

- Scientific notation is used to write very big or very small numbers in decimal form.

- In scientific notation, all numbers are written in the form of: $m \times 10^n$, where m is greater than 1 and less than 10.

- To convert a number from scientific notation to standard form, move the decimal point to the left (if the exponent of ten is a negative number), or to the right (if the exponent is positive).

Examples:

Example 1. Write 0.00024 in scientific notation.

Solution: First, move the decimal point to the right so you have a number between 1 and 10. That number is 2.4. Now, determine how many places the decimal moved in step 1 by the power of 10. We moved the decimal point 4 digits to the right. Then: $10^{-4} \rightarrow$ When the decimal moved to the right, the exponent is negative. Then: $0.00024 = 2.4 \times 10^{-4}$

Example 2. Write 3.8×10^{-5} in standard notation.

Solution: $10^{-5} \rightarrow$ When the decimal moved to the right, the exponent is negative. Then: $3.8 \times 10^{-5} = 0.000038$

Example 3. Write 0.00031 in scientific notation.

Solution: First, move the decimal point to the right so you have a number between 1 and 10. Then: $m = 3.1$, Now, determine how many places the decimal moved in step 1 by the power of 10.
$10^{-4} \rightarrow$ Then: $0.00031 = 3.1 \times 10^{-4}$

Example 4. Write 6.2×10^5 in standard notation.

Solution: $10^5 \rightarrow$ The exponent is positive 5. Then, move the decimal point to the right five digits. (remember $6.2 = 6.20000$),
Then: $6.2 \times 10^5 = 620,000$

bit.ly/3nOwJYP

Find more at

Radicals

- If n is a positive integer and x is a real number, then: $\sqrt[n]{x} = x^{\frac{1}{n}}$,

$$\sqrt[n]{xy} = x^{\frac{1}{n}} \times y^{\frac{1}{n}}, \sqrt[n]{\frac{x}{y}} = \frac{x^{\frac{1}{n}}}{y^{\frac{1}{n}}}, \text{ and } \sqrt[n]{x} \times \sqrt[n]{y} = \sqrt[n]{xy}$$

- A square root of x is a number r whose square is: $r^2 = x$ (r is a square root of x)

- To add and subtract radicals, we need to have the same values under the radical. For example: $\sqrt{3} + \sqrt{3} = 2\sqrt{3}$, $3\sqrt{5} - \sqrt{5} = 2\sqrt{5}$

Examples:

Example 1. Find the square root of $\sqrt{121}$.

Solution: First, factor the number: $121 = 11^2$, Then: $\sqrt{121} = \sqrt{11^2}$,
Now use radical rule: $\sqrt[n]{a^n} = a$. Then: $\sqrt{121} = \sqrt{11^2} = 11$

Example 2. Evaluate. $\sqrt{4} \times \sqrt{16} =$

Solution: Find the values of $\sqrt{4}$ and $\sqrt{16}$. Then: $\sqrt{4} \times \sqrt{16} = 2 \times 4 = 8$

Example 3. Solve. $5\sqrt{2} + 9\sqrt{2}$.

Solution: Since we have the same values under the radical, we can add these two radicals: $5\sqrt{2} + 9\sqrt{2} = 14\sqrt{2}$

Example 4. Evaluate. $\sqrt{2} \times \sqrt{50} =$

Solution: Use this radical rule: $\sqrt[n]{x} \times \sqrt[n]{y} = \sqrt[n]{xy} \rightarrow \sqrt{2} \times \sqrt{50} = \sqrt{100}$
The square root of 100 is 10. Then: $\sqrt{2} \times \sqrt{50} = \sqrt{100} = 10$

Chapter 6: Practices

✎ Find the products.

1) $x^2 \times 4xy^2 =$

2) $3x^2y \times 5x^3y^2 =$

3) $6x^4y^2 \times x^2y^3 =$

4) $7xy^3 \times 2x^2y =$

5) $-5x^5y^5 \times x^3y^2 =$

6) $-8x^3y^2 \times 3x^3y^2 =$

7) $-6x^2y^6 \times 5x^4y^2 =$

8) $-3x^3y^3 \times 2x^3y^2 =$

9) $-6x^5y^3 \times 4x^4y^3 =$

10) $-2x^4y^3 \times 5x^6y^2 =$

11) $-7y^6 \times 3x^6y^3 =$

12) $-9x^4 \times 2x^4y^2 =$

✎ Simplify.

13) $\frac{5^3 \times 5^4}{5^9 \times 5} =$

14) $\frac{3^3 \times 3^2}{7^2 \times 7} =$

15) $\frac{15x^5}{5x^3} =$

16) $\frac{16x^3}{4x^5} =$

17) $\frac{72y^2}{8x^3y^6} =$

18) $\frac{10x^3y^4}{50x^2y^3} =$

19) $\frac{13y^2}{52x^4y^4} =$

20) $\frac{50xy^3}{200x^3y^4} =$

21) $\frac{48x^2}{56x^2y^2} =$

22) $\frac{81y^6x}{54x^4y^3} =$

✎ Solve.

23) $(x^3y^3)^2 =$

24) $(3x^3y^4)^3 =$

25) $(4x \times 6xy^3)^2 =$

26) $(5x \times 2y^3)^3 =$

27) $\left(\frac{9x}{x^3}\right)^2 =$

28) $\left(\frac{3y}{18y^2}\right)^2 =$

29) $\left(\frac{3x^2y^3}{24x^4y^2}\right)^3 =$

30) $\left(\frac{26x^5y^3}{52x^3y^5}\right)^2 =$

31) $\left(\frac{18x^7y^4}{72x^5y^2}\right)^2 =$

32) $\left(\frac{12x^6y^4}{48x^5y^3}\right)^2 =$

Effortless Math Education

✍ **Evaluate each expression. (Zero and Negative Exponents)**

33) $\left(\frac{1}{4}\right)^{-2} =$

34) $\left(\frac{1}{3}\right)^{-2} =$

35) $\left(\frac{1}{7}\right)^{-3} =$

36) $\left(\frac{2}{5}\right)^{-3} =$

37) $\left(\frac{2}{3}\right)^{-3} =$

38) $\left(\frac{3}{5}\right)^{-4} =$

✍ **Write each expression with positive exponents.**

39) $x^{-7} =$

40) $3y^{-5} =$

41) $15y^{-3} =$

42) $-20x^{-4} =$

43) $12a^{-3}b^5 =$

44) $25a^3b^{-4}c^{-3} =$

45) $-4x^5y^{-3}z^{-6} =$

46) $\frac{18y}{x^3y^{-2}} =$

47) $\frac{20a^{-2}b}{-12c^{-4}}$

✍ **Write each number in scientific notation.**

48) $0.00412 =$

49) $0.000053 =$

50) $66,000 =$

51) $72,000,000 =$

✍ **Evaluate.**

52) $\sqrt{8} \times \sqrt{8} =$ ....

53) $\sqrt{36} - \sqrt{9} =$ ....

54) $\sqrt{81} + \sqrt{16} =$

55) $\sqrt{4} \times \sqrt{25} =$ ....

56) $\sqrt{2} \times \sqrt{32} =$ ....

57) $4\sqrt{3} + 5\sqrt{3} =$ ....

Effortless
Math
Education

EffortlessMath.com

Chapter 6: Answers

1) $4x^3y^2$

2) $15x^5y^3$

3) $6x^6y^5$

4) $14x^3y^4$

5) $-5x^8y^7$

6) $-24x^6y^4$

7) $-30x^6y^8$

8) $-6x^6y^5$

9) $-24x^9y^6$

10) $-10x^{10}y^5$

11) $-21x^6y^9$

12) $-18x^8y^2$

13) $\frac{1}{125}$

14) $\frac{243}{343}$

15) $3x^2$

16) $\frac{4}{x^2}$

17) $\frac{9}{x^3y^4}$

18) $\frac{xy}{5}$

19) $\frac{1}{4x^4y^2}$

20) $\frac{1}{4x^2y}$

21) $\frac{6}{7y^2}$

22) $\frac{3y^3}{2x^3}$

23) x^6y^6

24) $27x^9y^{12}$

25) $576x^4y^6$

26) $1,000x^3y^9$

27) $\frac{81}{x^4}$

28) $\frac{1}{36y^2}$

29) $\frac{y^3}{512x^6}$

30) $\frac{x^4}{4y^4}$

31) $\frac{x^4y^4}{16}$

32) $\frac{x^2y^2}{16}$

33) 16

34) 9

35) 343

36) $\frac{125}{8}$

37) $\frac{27}{8}$

38) $\frac{625}{81}$

39) $\frac{1}{x^7}$

40) $\frac{3}{y^5}$

41) $\frac{15}{y^3}$

42) $-\frac{20}{x^4}$

43) $\frac{12b^5}{a^3}$

44) $\frac{25a^3}{b^4c^3}$

45) $-\frac{4x^5}{y^3z^6}$

46) $\frac{18y^3}{x^3}$

47) $-\frac{5bc^4}{3a^2}$

48) 4.12×10^{-3}

49) 5.3×10^{-5}

50) 6.6×10^4

51) 7.2×10^7

52) 8

53) 3

54) 13

55) 10

56) 8

57) $9\sqrt{3}$

Effortless Math Education

CHAPTER

7 Expressions and Variables

Math topics that you'll learn in this chapter:

- ☑ Simplifying Variable Expressions
- ☑ Simplifying Polynomial Expressions
- ☑ The Distributive Property
- ☑ Evaluating One Variable
- ☑ Evaluating Two Variables

Simplifying Variable Expressions

- In algebra, a variable is a letter used to stand for a number. The most common letters are $x, y, z, a, b, c, m, and\ n$.

- An algebraic expression is an expression that contains integers, variables, and math operations such as addition, subtraction, multiplication, division, etc.

- In an expression, we can combine "like" terms. (values with same variable and same power)

Examples:

Example 1. Simplify. $(4x + 2x + 4) =$

Solution: In this expression, there are three terms: $4x, 2x$, and 4. Two terms are "like terms": $4x$ and $2x$. Combine like terms. $4x + 2x = 6x$. Then: $(4x + 2x + 4) = 6x + 4$ (***remember you cannot combine variables and numbers.***)

Example 2. Simplify. $-2x^2 - 5x + 4x^2 - 9 =$

Solution: Combine "like" terms: $-2x^2 + 4x^2 = 2x^2$.
Then: $-2x^2 - 5x + 4x^2 - 9 = 2x^2 - 5x - 9$.

Example 3. Simplify. $(-8 + 6x^2 + 3x^2 + 9x) =$

Solution: Combine like terms. Then:
$(-8 + 6x^2 + 3x^2 + 9x) = 9x^2 + 9x - 8$

Example 4. Simplify. $-10x + 6x^2 - 3x + 9x^2 =$

Solution: Combine "like" terms: $-10x - 3x = -13x$, and $6x^2 + 9x^2 = 15x^2$
Then: $-10x + 6x^2 - 3x + 9x^2 = -13x + 15x^2$. Write in standard form (biggest powers first): $-13x + 15x^2 = 15x^2 - 13x$

Simplifying Polynomial Expressions

- In mathematics, a polynomial is an expression consisting of variables and coefficients that involves only the operations of addition, subtraction, multiplication, and non–negative integer exponents of variables. $P(x) = a_n x^n + a_{n-1} x^{n-1} + \dots + a_2 x^2 + a_1 x + a_0$

- Polynomials must always be simplified as much as possible. It means you must add together any like terms. (values with same variable and same power)

Examples:

Example 1. Simplify this Polynomial Expressions. $3x^2 - 6x^3 - 2x^3 + 4x^4$

Solution: Combine "like" terms: $-6x^3 - 2x^3 = -8x^3$
Then: $3x^2 - 6x^3 - 2x^3 + 4x^4 = 3x^2 - 8x^3 + 4x^4$
Now, write the expression in standard form: $4x^4 - 8x^3 + 3x^2$

Example 2. Simplify this expression. $(-5x^2 + 2x^3) - (3x^3 - 6x^2) =$

Solution: First, use distributive property: $\rightarrow$ multiply $(-)$ into $(3x^3 - 6x^2)$
$(-5x^2 + 2x^3) - (3x^3 - 6x^2) = -5x^2 + 2x^3 - 3x^3 + 6x^2$
Then combine "like" terms: $-5x^2 + 2x^3 - 3x^3 + 6x^2 = x^2 - x^3$
And write in standard form: $x^2 - x^3 = -x^3 + x^2$

Example 3. Simplify. $3x^3 - 9x^4 - 8x^2 + 12x^4 =$

Solution: Combine "like" terms:
$-9x^4 + 12x^4 = 3x^4$
Then: $3x^3 - 9x^4 - 8x^2 + 12x^4 = 3x^3 + 3x^4 - 8x^2$
And write in standard form: $3x^3 + 3x^4 - 8x^2 = 3x^4 + 3x^3 - 8x^2$

bit.ly/2WT5gtn

Find more at

The Distributive Property

- The distributive property (or the distributive property of multiplication over addition and subtraction) simplifies and solves expressions in the form of: $a(b + c)$ or $a(b - c)$

- The distributive property is multiplying a term outside the parentheses by the terms inside.

- Distributive Property rule: $a(b + c) = ab + ac$

Examples:

Example 1. Simply using the distributive property. $(-2)(x + 3)$

Solution: Use Distributive Property rule: $a(b + c) = ab + ac$
$(-2)(x + 3) = (-2 \times x) + (-2) \times (3) = -2x - 6$

Example 2. Simply. $(-5)(-2x - 6)$

Solution: Use Distributive Property rule: $a(b + c) = ab + ac$
$(-5)(-2x - 6) = (-5 \times -2x) + (-5) \times (-6) = 10x + 30$

Example 3. Simply. $(7)(2x - 8) - 12x$

Solution: First, simplify $(7)(2x - 8)$ using the distributive property.
Then: $(7)(2x - 8) = 14x - 56$
Now combine like terms: $(7)(2x - 8) - 12x = 14x - 56 - 12x$
In this expression, $14x$ and $-12x$ are "like terms" and we can combine them.
$14x - 12x = 2x$. Then: $14x - 56 - 12x = 2x - 56$

Evaluating One Variable

- To evaluate one variable expression, find the variable and substitute a number for that variable.

- Perform the arithmetic operations.

Examples:

Example 1. Calculate this expression for $x = 2$. $8 + 2x$

Solution: First, substitute 2 for x.
Then: $8 + 2x = 8 + 2(2)$
Now, use order of operation to find the answer: $8 + 2(2) = 8 + 4 = 12$

Example 2. Evaluate this expression for $x = -1$. $4x - 8$

Solution: First, substitute -1 for x,
Then: $4x - 8 = 4(-1) - 8$
Now, use order of operation to find the answer: $4(-1) - 8 = -4 - 8 = -12$

Example 3. Find the value of this expression when $x = 4$. $16 - 5x$

Solution: First, substitute 4 for x,
Then: $16 - 5x = 16 - 5(4) = 16 - 20 = -4$

Example 4. Solve this expression for $x = -3$. $15 + 7x$

Solution: Substitute -3 for x,
Then: $15 + 7x = 15 + 7(-3) = 15 - 21 = -6$

Evaluating Two Variables

- To evaluate an algebraic expression, substitute a number for each variable.

- Perform the arithmetic operations to find the value of the expression.

Examples:

Example 1. Calculate this expression for a = 2 and $b = -1$. $4a - 3b$

Solution: First, substitute 2 for a, and -1 for b ,
Then: $4a - 3b = 4(2) - 3(-1)$
Now, use order of operation to find the answer: $4(2) - 3(-1) = 8 + 3 = 11$

Example 2. Evaluate this expression for $x = -2$ and $y = 2$. $3x + 6y$

Solution: Substitute -2 for x, and 2 for y ,
Then: $3x + 6y = 3(-2) + 6(2) = -6 + 12 = 6$

Example 3. Find the value of this expression $2(6a - 5b)$ when $a = -1$ and $b = 4$.

Solution: Substitute -1 for a, and 4 for b ,
Then: $2(6a - 5b) = 12a - 10b = 12(-1) - 10(4) = -12 - 40 = -52$

Example 4. Solve this expression. $-7x - 2y, \ x = 4, \ y = -3$

Solution: Substitute 4 for x, and -3 for y and simplify.
Then: $-7x - 2y = -7(4) - 2(-3) = -28 + 6 = -22$

Chapter 7: Practices

✎ Simplify each expression.

1) $(3 + 4x - 1) =$

2) $(-5 - 2x + 7) =$

3) $(12x - 5x - 4) =$

4) $(-16x + 24x - 9) =$

5) $(6x + 5 - 15x) =$

6) $2 + 5x - 8x - 6 =$

7) $5x + 10 - 3x - 22 =$

8) $-5 - 3x^2 - 6 + 4x =$

9) $-6 + 9x^2 - 3 + x =$

10) $5x^2 + 3x - 10x - 3 =$

11) $4x^2 - 2x - 6x + 5 - 8 =$

12) $3x^2 - 5x - 7x + 2 - 4 =$

13) $9x^2 - x - 5x + 3 - 9 =$

14) $2x^2 - 7x - 3x^2 + 4x + 6 =$

✎ Simplify each polynomial.

15) $5x^2 + 3x^3 - 9x^2 + 2x =$

16) $8x^4 + 2x^5 - 7x^4 + 3x^2 =$

17) $15x^3 + 11x - 5x^2 - 9x^3 =$

18) $(7x^3 - 3x^2) + (5x^2 - 13x) =$

19) $(12x^4 + 6x^3) + (x^3 - 5x^4) =$

20) $(15x^5 - 8x^3) - (4x^3 + x^2) =$

21) $(14x^4 + 7x^3) - (x^3 - 24) =$

22) $(20x^4 + 6x^3) - (-x^3 - 2x^4) =$

23) $(x^2 + 9x^3) + (-22x^2 + 6x^3) =$

24) $(4x^4 - 2x^3) + (-5x^3 - 8x^4) =$

Effortless Math Education

✎ **Use the distributive property to simply each expression.**

25) $2(6 + x) =$ _____

26) $5(3 - 2x) =$ _____

27) $7(1 - 5x) =$ _____

28) $(3 - 4x)7 =$ _____

29) $6(2 - 3x) =$ _____

30) $(-1)(-9 + x) =$ _____

31) $(-6)(3x - 2) =$ _____

32) $(-x + 12)(-4) =$ _____

33) $(-2)(1 - 6x) =$ _____

34) $(-5x - 3)(-8) =$ _____

✎ **Evaluate each expression using the value given.**

35) $x = 4 \to 10 - x =$ ____

36) $x = 6 \to x + 8 =$ ____

37) $x = 3 \to 2x - 6 =$ ____

38) $x = 2 \to 10 - 4x =$ ____

39) $x = 7 \to 8x - 3 =$ ____

40) $x = 9 \to 20 - 2x =$ ____

41) $x = 5 \to 10x - 30 =$ ___

42) $x = -6 \to 5 - x =$ ____

43) $x = -3 \to 22 - 3x =$ ____

44) $x = -7 \to 10 - 9x =$ ____

45) $x = -10 \to 40 - 3x =$ ____

46) $x = -2 \to 20x - 5 =$ ____

47) $x = -5 \to -10x - 8 =$ ___

48) $x = -4 \to -1 - 4x =$ ___

✎ **Evaluate each expression using the values given.**

49) $x = 2, y = 1 \to 2x + 7y =$ _____

50) $a = 3, b = 5 \to 3a - 5b =$ _____

51) $x = 6, y = 2 \to 3x - 2y + 8 =$ _____

52) $a = -2, b = 3 \to -5a + 2b + 6 =$ _____

53) $x = -4, y = -3 \to -4x + 10 - 8y =$ _____

Effortless
Math
Education

Effortless
Math
Education

Chapter 7: Answers

1) $4x + 2$

2) $-2x + 2$

3) $7x - 4$

4) $8x - 9$

5) $-9x + 5$

6) $-3x - 4$

7) $2x - 12$

8) $-3x^2 + 4x - 11$

9) $9x^2 + x - 9$

10) $5x^2 - 7x - 3$

11) $4x^2 - 8x - 3$

12) $3x^2 - 12x - 2$

13) $9x^2 - 6x - 6$

14) $-x^2 - 3x + 6$

15) $3x^3 - 4x^2 + 2x$

16) $2x^5 + x^4 + 3x^2$

17) $6x^3 - 5x^2 + 11x$

18) $7x^3 + 2x^2 - 13x$

19) $7x^4 + 7x^3$

20) $15x^5 - 12x^3 - x^2$

21) $14x^4 + 6x^3 + 24$

22) $22x^4 + 7x^3$

23) $15x^3 - 21x^2$

24) $-4x^4 - 7x^3$

25) $2x + 12$

26) $-10x + 15$

27) $-35x + 7$

28) $-28x + 21$

29) $-18x + 12$

30) $-x + 9$

31) $-18x + 12$

32) $4x - 48$

33) $12x - 2$

34) $40x + 24$

35) 6

36) 14

37) 0

38) 2

39) 53

40) 2

41) 20

42) 11

43) 31

44) 73

45) 70

46) -45

47) 42

48) 15

49) 11

50) -16

51) 22

52) 22

53) 50

Effortless
Math
Education

CHAPTER

8 Equations and Inequalities

Math topics that you'll learn in this chapter:

- ☑ One-Step Equations
- ☑ Multi-Step Equations
- ☑ System of Equations
- ☑ Graphing Single–Variable Inequalities
- ☑ One-Step Inequalities
- ☑ Multi-Step Inequalities

One−Step Equations

- The values of two expressions on both sides of an equation are equal. Example: $ax = b$. In this equation, ax is equal to b.

- Solving an equation means finding the value of the variable.

- You only need to perform one Math operation to solve the one-step equations.

- To solve a one-step equation, find the inverse (opposite) operation is being performed.

- The inverse operations are:

  ❖ Addition and subtraction
  ❖ Multiplication and division

Examples:

Example 1. Solve this equation for x. $4x = 16, x = ?$

Solution: Here, the operation is multiplication (variable x is multiplied by 4) and its inverse operation is division. To solve this equation, divide both sides of equation by 4: $4x = 16 \rightarrow \frac{4x}{4} = \frac{16}{4} \rightarrow x = 4$

Example 2. Solve this equation. $x + 8 = 0$, $x = ?$

Solution: In this equation 8 is added to the variable x. The inverse operation of addition is subtraction. To solve this equation, subtract 8 from both sides of the equation: $x + 8 - 8 = 0 - 8$. Then: $\rightarrow x = -8$

Example 3. Solve this equation for x. $x - 12 = 0$

Solution: Here, the operation is subtraction and its inverse operation is addition. To solve this equation, add 12 to both sides of the equation: $x - 12 + 12 = 0 + 12 \rightarrow x = 12$

Multi−Step Equations

- To solve a multi-step equation, combine "like" terms on one side.

- Bring variables to one side by adding or subtracting.

- Simplify using the inverse of addition or subtraction.

- Simplify further by using the inverse of multiplication or division.

- Check your solution by plugging the value of the variable into the original equation.

Examples:

Example 1. Solve this equation for x. $4x + 8 = 20 - 2x$

Solution: First, bring variables to one side by adding $2x$ to both sides. Then: $4x + 8 + 2x = 20 - 2x + 2x \rightarrow 4x + 8 + 2x = 20$.

Simplify: $6x + 8 = 20$ Now, subtract 8 from both sides of the equation:

$6x + 8 - 8 = 20 - 8 \rightarrow 6x = 12 \rightarrow$ Divide both sides by 6:

$6x = 12 \rightarrow \dfrac{6x}{6} = \dfrac{12}{6} \rightarrow x = 2$

Let's check this solution by substituting the value of 2 for x in the original equation:

$x = 2 \rightarrow 4x + 8 = 20 - 2x \rightarrow 4(2) + 8 = 20 - 2(2) \rightarrow 16 = 16$

The answer $x = 2$ is correct.

Example 2. Solve this equation for x. $-5x + 4 = 24$

Solution: Subtract 4 from both sides of the equation.

$-5x + 4 = 24 \rightarrow -5x + 4 - 4 = 24 - 4 \rightarrow -5x = 20$

Divide both sides by -5, then: $-5x = 20 \rightarrow \dfrac{-5x}{-5} = \dfrac{20}{-5} \rightarrow x = -4$

Now, check the solution:

$x = -4 \rightarrow -5x + 4 = 24 \rightarrow -5(-4) + 4 = 24 \rightarrow 24 = 24$

The answer $x = -4$ is correct.

bit.ly/3nQbSEB

Find more at

System of Equations

- A system of equations contains two equations and two variables. For example, consider the system of equations: $x - y = 1, x + y = 5$

- The easiest way to solve a system of equations is using the elimination method. The elimination method uses the addition property of equality. You can add the same value to each side of an equation.

- For the first equation above, you can add $x + y$ to the left side and 5 to the right side of the first equation: $x - y + (x + y) = 1 + 5$. Now, if you simplify, you get: $x - y + (x + y) = 1 + 5 \rightarrow 2x = 6 \rightarrow x = 3$. Now, substitute 3 for the x in the first equation: $3 - y = 1$. By solving this equation, $y = 2$

Example:

What is the value of $x + y$ in this system of equations?

$$\begin{cases} 2x + 4y = 12 \\ 4x - 2y = -16 \end{cases}$$

Solution: Solving a System of Equations by Elimination:
Multiply the first equation by (-2), then add it to the second equation.

$$\begin{array}{r} -2(2x + 4y = 12) \\ 4x - 2y = -16 \end{array} \Rightarrow \begin{array}{r} -4x - 8y = -24 \\ 4x - 2y = -16 \end{array} \Rightarrow -10y = -40 \Rightarrow y = 4$$

Plug in the value of y into one of the equations and solve for x.
$2x + 4(4) = 12 \Rightarrow 2x + 16 = 12 \Rightarrow 2x = -4 \Rightarrow x = -2$
Thus, $x + y = -2 + 4 = 2$

Graphing Single–Variable Inequalities

- An inequality compares two expressions using an inequality sign.

- Inequality signs are: "less than" <, "greater than" >, "less than or equal to" ≤, and "greater than or equal to" ≥.

- To graph a single–variable inequality, find the value of the inequality on the number line.

- For less than (<) or greater than (>) draw an open circle on the value of the variable. If there is an equal sign too, then use a filled circle.

- Draw an arrow to the right for greater or to the left for less than.

Examples:

Example 1. Draw a graph for this inequality. $x > 2$

Solution: Since the variable is greater than 2, then we need to find 2 in the number line and draw an open circle on it. Then, draw an arrow to the right.

Example 2. Graph this inequality. $x \leq -3$.

Solution: Since the variable is less than or equal to -3, then we need to find -3 in the number line and draw a filled circle on it. Then, draw an arrow to the left.

bit.ly/3aJ4GGo

Find more at

One–Step Inequalities

- An inequality compares two expressions using an inequality sign.

- Inequality signs are: "less than" $<$, "greater than" $>$, "less than or equal to" $\leq$, and "greater than or equal to" $\geq$.

- You only need to perform one Math operation to solve the one-step inequalities.

- To solve one-step inequalities, find the inverse (opposite) operation is being performed.

- For dividing or multiplying both sides by negative numbers, flip the direction of the inequality sign.

Examples:

Example 1. Solve this inequality for x. $x + 5 \geq 4$

Solution: The inverse (opposite) operation of addition is subtraction. In this inequality, 5 is added to x. To isolate x we need to subtract 5 from both sides of the inequality.
Then: $x + 5 \geq 4 \rightarrow x + 5 - 5 \geq 4 - 5 \rightarrow x \geq -1$. The solution is: $x \geq -1$

Example 2. Solve the inequality. $x - 3 > -6$.

Solution: 3 is subtracted from x. Add 3 to both sides.
$x - 3 > -6 \rightarrow x - 3 + 3 > -6 + 3 \rightarrow x > -3$

Example 3. Solve. $4x \leq -8$.

Solution: 4 is multiplied to x. Divide both sides by 4.
Then: $4x \leq -8 \rightarrow \frac{4x}{4} \leq \frac{-8}{4} \rightarrow x \leq -2$

Example 4. Solve. $-3x \leq 6$.

Solution: -3 is multiplied to x. Divide both sides by -3. Remember when dividing or multiplying both sides of an inequality by negative numbers, flip the direction of the inequality sign.
Then: $-3x \leq 6 \rightarrow \frac{-3x}{-3} \geq \frac{6}{-3} \rightarrow x \geq -2$

Multi–Step Inequalities

- To solve a multi-step inequality, combine "like" terms on one side.

- Bring variables to one side by adding or subtracting.

- Isolate the variable.

- Simplify using the inverse of addition or subtraction.

- Simplify further by using the inverse of multiplication or division.

- For dividing or multiplying both sides by negative numbers, flip the direction of the inequality sign.

Examples:

Example 1. Solve this inequality. $8x - 2 \leq 14$

Solution: In this inequality, 2 is subtracted from $8x$. The inverse of subtraction is addition. Add 2 to both sides of the inequality:
$8x - 2 + 2 \leq 14 + 2 \rightarrow 8x \leq 16$
Now, divide both sides by 8. Then: $8x \leq 16 \rightarrow \frac{8x}{8} \leq \frac{16}{8} \rightarrow x \leq 2$

The solution of this inequality is $x \leq 2$.

Example 2. Solve this inequality. $3x + 9 < 12$

Solution: First, subtract 9 from both sides: $3x + 9 - 9 < 12 - 9$
Then simplify: $3x + 9 - 9 < 12 - 9 \rightarrow 3x < 3$
Now divide both sides by 3: $\frac{3x}{3} < \frac{3}{3} \rightarrow x < 1$

Example 3. Solve this inequality. $-5x + 3 \geq 8$

Solution: First, subtract 3 from both sides:
$-5x + 3 - 3 \geq 8 - 3 \rightarrow -5x \geq 5$
Divide both sides by -5. Remember that you need to flip the direction of inequality sign. $-5x \geq 5 \rightarrow \frac{-5x}{-5} \leq \frac{5}{-5} \rightarrow x \leq -1$

bit.ly/2WK1xOr

Find more at

Chapter 8: Practices

✎ Solve each equation. (One–Step Equations)

1) $x + 6 = 3 \rightarrow x =$ _____

2) $5 = 11 - x \rightarrow x =$ _____

3) $-3 = 8 + x \rightarrow x =$ _____

4) $x - 2 = -7 \rightarrow x =$ _____

5) $-15 = x + 6 \rightarrow x =$ _____

6) $10 - x = -2 \rightarrow x =$ _____

7) $22 - x = -9 \rightarrow x =$ _____

8) $-4 + x = 28 \rightarrow x =$ _____

9) $11 - x = -7 \rightarrow x =$ _____

10) $35 - x = -7 \rightarrow x =$ _____

✎ Solve each equation. (Multi–Step Equations)

11) $4(x + 2) = 12 \rightarrow x =$ _____

12) $-6(6 - x) = 12 \rightarrow x =$ _____

13) $5 = -5(x + 2) \rightarrow x =$ _____

14) $-10 = 2(4 + x) \rightarrow x =$ _____

15) $4(x + 2) = -12, x =$ _____

16) $-6(3 + 2x) = 30, x =$ _____

17) $-3(4 - x) = 12, x =$ _____

18) $-4(6 - x) = 16, x =$ _____

✎ Solve each system of equations.

19) $\begin{cases} x + 6y = 32 \\ x + 3y = 17 \end{cases}$ $x =$ _____ $y =$ _____

20) $\begin{cases} 3x + y = 15 \\ x + 2y = 10 \end{cases}$ $x =$ _____ $y =$ _____

21) $\begin{cases} 3x + 5y = 17 \\ 2x + y = 9 \end{cases}$ $x =$ _____ $y =$ _____

22) $\begin{cases} 5x - 2y = -8 \\ -6x + 2y = 10 \end{cases}$ $x =$ _____ $y =$ _____

Effortless
Math
Education

✎ **Draw a graph for each inequality.**

23) $x \leq -3$

24) $x > -5$

✎ **Solve each inequality and graph it.**

25) $x - 2 \geq -2$

26) $2x - 3 < 9$

✎ **Solve each inequality.**

27) $x + 13 > 4$ 36) $6(6 + x) \geq -18$

28) $x + 6 > 5$ 37) $2(x - 5) \geq -14$

29) $-12 + 2x \leq 26$ 38) $6(x + 4) < -12$

30) $-2 + 8x \leq 14$ 39) $3(x - 8) \geq -48$

31) $6 + 4x \leq 18$ 40) $-(6 - 4x) > -30$

32) $4(x + 3) \geq -12$ 41) $2(2 + 2x) > -60$

33) $2(6 + x) \geq -12$ 42) $-3(4 + 2x) > -24$

34) $3(x - 5) < -6$

35) $10 + 5x < -15$

Effortless
Math
Education

Chapter 8: Answers

1) -3

2) 6

3) -11

4) -5

5) -21

6) 12

7) 31

8) 32

9) 18

10) 42

11) 1

12) 8

13) -3

14) -9

15) -5

16) -4

17) 8

18) 10

19) $x = 2, y = 5$

20) $x = 4, y = 3$

21) $x = 4, y = 1$

22) $x = -2, y = -1$

23) $x \le -3$

24) $x > -5$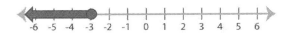

25) $x \ge 0$

26) $x < 6$

27) $x > -9$

28) $x > -1$

29) $x \le 19$

30) $x \le 2$

31) $x \le 3$

32) $x \ge -6$

33) $x \ge -12$

34) $x < 3$

35) $x < -5$

36) $x \ge -9$

37) $x \ge -2$

38) $x < -6$

39) $x \ge -8$

40) $x > -6$

41) $x > -16$

42) $x < 2$

CHAPTER

9 Lines and Slope

Math topics that you'll learn in this chapter:

☑ Finding Slope

☑ Graphing Lines Using Slope–Intercept Form

☑ Writing Linear Equations

☑ Finding Midpoint

☑ Finding Distance of Two Points

☑ Graphing Linear Inequalities

Finding Slope

- The slope of a line represents the direction of a line on the coordinate plane.

- A coordinate plane contains two perpendicular number lines. The horizontal line is x and the vertical line is y. The point at which the two axes intersect is called the origin. An ordered pair (x, y) shows the location of a point.

- A line on a coordinate plane can be drawn by connecting two points.

- To find the slope of a line, we need the equation of the line or two points on the line.

- The slope of a line with two points A (x_1, y_1) and B (x_2, y_2) can be found by using this formula: $\frac{y_2 - y_1}{x_2 - x_1} = \frac{rise}{run}$

- The equation of a line is typically written as $y = mx + b$ where m is the slope and b is the y-intercept.

Examples:

Example 1. Find the slope of the line through these two points:

A$(1, -6)$ *and* $B(3, 2)$.

Solution: Slope $= \frac{y_2 - y_1}{x_2 - x_1}$. Let (x_1, y_1) be A$(1, -6)$ and (x_2, y_2) be $B(3, 2)$.

(Remember, you can choose any point for (x_1, y_1) and (x_2, y_2)).

Then: slope $= \frac{y_2 - y_1}{x_2 - x_1} = \frac{2-(-6)}{3-1} = \frac{8}{2} = 4$

The slope of the line through these two points is 4.

Example 2. Find the slope of the line with equation $y = -2x + 8$

Solution: when the equation of a line is written in the form of $y = mx + b$, the slope is m. In this line: $y = -2x + 8$, the slope is -2.

Graphing Lines Using Slope–Intercept Form

- Slope–intercept form of a line: given the slope **m** and the **y**–intercept (the intersection of the line and y-axis) **b**, then the equation of the line is:

$$y = mx + b$$

- To draw the graph of a linear equation in a slope-intercept form on the xy coordinate plane, find two points on the line by plugging two values for x and calculating the values of y.

- You can also use the slope (m) and one point to graph the line.

Example:

Sketch the graph of $y = 2x - 4$.

Solution: To graph this line, we need to find two points. When x is zero the value of y is -4. And when x is 2 the value of y is 0.

$$x = 0 \rightarrow y = 2(0) - 4 = -4,$$
$$y = 0 \rightarrow 0 = 2x - 4 \rightarrow x = 2$$

Now, we have two points:
$(0, -4)$ and $(2, 0)$.
Find the points on the coordinate plane and graph the line. Remember that the slope of the line is 2.

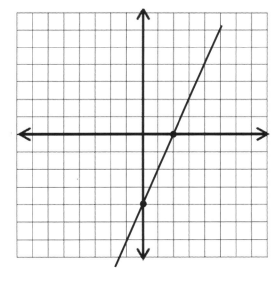

Writing Linear Equations

- The equation of a line in slope-intercept form: $y = mx + b$

- To write the equation of a line, first identify the slope.

- Find the y-intercept. This can be done by substituting the slope and the coordinates of a point (x, y) on the line.

Examples:

Example 1. What is the equation of the line that passes through $(3, -4)$ and has a slope of 6?

Solution: The general slope-intercept form of the equation of a line is $y = mx + b$, where m is the slope and b is the y-intercept.
By substitution of the given point and given slope:
$y = mx + b \rightarrow -4 = (3)(6) + b$. So, $b = -4 - 18 = -22$, and the required equation is $y = 6x - 22$

Example 2. Write the equation of the line through two points $A(3,1)$ and $B(-2, 6)$.

Solution: First, find the slope: $Slop = \frac{y_2 - y_1}{x_2 - x_1} = \frac{6 - 1}{-2 - 3} = \frac{5}{-5} = -1 \rightarrow m = -1$

To find the value of b, use either points and plug in the values of x and y in the equation. The answer will be the same: $y = -x + b$. Let's check both points. Then: $(3,1) \rightarrow y = mx + b \rightarrow 1 = -1(3) + b \rightarrow b = 4$
$(-2,6) \rightarrow y = mx + b \rightarrow 6 = -1(-2) + b \rightarrow b = 4$.
The y-intercept of the line is 4. The equation of the line is: $y = -x + 4$

Example 3. What is the equation of the line that passes through $(4, -1)$ and has a slope of 4?

Solution: The general slope-intercept form of the equation of a line is $y = mx + b$, where m is the slope and b is the y-intercept. By substitution of the given point and given slope:$y = mx + b \rightarrow -1 = (4)(4) + b$

So, $b = -1 - 16 = -17$, and the equation of the line is: $y = 4x - 17$.

Finding Midpoint

- The middle of a line segment is its midpoint.

- The Midpoint of two endpoints A (x_1, y_1) and B (x_2, y_2) can be found using this formula: M $(\frac{x_1+x_2}{2}, \frac{y_1+y_2}{2})$

Examples:

Example 1. Find the midpoint of the line segment with the given endpoints. $(2, -4), (6, 8)$

Solution: Midpoint $= \left(\frac{x_1+x_2}{2}, \frac{y_1+y_2}{2}\right) \rightarrow (x_1, y_1) = (2, -4)$ and $(x_2, y_2) = (6, 8)$
Midpoint $= \left(\frac{2+6}{2}, \frac{-4+8}{2}\right) \rightarrow \left(\frac{8}{2}, \frac{4}{2}\right) \rightarrow M(4, 2)$

Example 2. Find the midpoint of the line segment with the given endpoints. $(-2, 3), (6, -7)$

Solution: Midpoint $= \left(\frac{x_1+x_2}{2}, \frac{y_1+y_2}{2}\right) \rightarrow (x_1, y_1) = (-2, 3)$ and $(x_2, y_2) = (6, -7)$
Midpoint $= \left(\frac{-2+6}{2}, \frac{3-7}{2}\right) \rightarrow \left(\frac{4}{2}, \frac{-4}{2}\right) \rightarrow M(2, -2)$

Example 3. Find the midpoint of the line segment with the given endpoints. $(7, -4), (1, 8)$

Solution: Midpoint $= \left(\frac{x_1+x_2}{2}, \frac{y_1+y_2}{2}\right) \rightarrow (x_1, y_1) = (7, -4)$ and $(x_2, y_2) = (1, 8)$
Midpoint $= \left(\frac{7+1}{2}, \frac{-4+8}{2}\right) \rightarrow \left(\frac{8}{2}, \frac{4}{2}\right) \rightarrow M(4, 2)$

Example 4. Find the midpoint of the line segment with the given endpoints. $(6, 3), (10, -9)$

Solution: Midpoint $= \left(\frac{x_1+x_2}{2}, \frac{y_1+y_2}{2}\right) \rightarrow (x_1, y_1) = (6, 3)$ and $(x_2, y_2) = (10, -9)$
Midpoint $= \left(\frac{6+10}{2}, \frac{3-9}{2}\right) \rightarrow \left(\frac{16}{2}, \frac{-6}{2}\right) \rightarrow M(8, -3)$

bit.ly/3nPdnTq

Find more at

Finding Distance of Two Points

- Use the following formula to find the distance of two points with the coordinates A (x_1, y_1) and B (x_2, y_2):

$$d = \sqrt{(x_2 - x_1)^2 + (y_2 - y_1)^2}$$

Examples:

Example 1. Find the distance between $(4, 2)$ and $(-5, -10)$.

Solution: Use distance of two points formula: $d = \sqrt{(x_2 - x_1)^2 + (y_2 - y_1)^2}$
$(x_1, y_1) = (4, 2)$ and $(x_2, y_2) = (-5, -10)$. Then: $d = \sqrt{(x_2 - x_1)^2 + (y_2 - y_1)^2} \rightarrow$
$= \sqrt{(-5 - 4)^2 + (-10 - 2)^2} = \sqrt{(-9)^2 + (-12)^2} = \sqrt{81 + 144} = \sqrt{225} = 15$
Then: $d = 15$

Example 2. Find the distance of two points $(-1, 5)$ and $(-3, -6)$.

Solution: Use distance of two points formula: $d = \sqrt{(x_2 - x_1)^2 + (y_2 - y_1)^2}$
$(x_1, y_1) = (-1, 5)$, and $(x_2, y_2) = (-3, -6)$
Then: $= \sqrt{(x_2 - x_1)^2 + (y_2 - y_1)^2} \rightarrow d = \sqrt{(-3 - (-1))^2 + (-6 - (5))^2} =$
$\sqrt{(-2)^2 + (-11)^2} = \sqrt{4 + 121} = \sqrt{125} = 5\sqrt{5}$. Then: $d = 5\sqrt{5}$

Example 3. Find the distance between $(-6, 5)$ and $(-2, 2)$.

Solution: Use distance of two points formula: $d = \sqrt{(x_2 - x_1)^2 + (y_2 - y_1)^2}$
$(x_1, y_1) = (-6, 5)$ and $(x_2, y_2) = (-2, 2)$. Then: $d = \sqrt{(x_2 - x_1)^2 + (y_2 - y_1)^2}$
$$d = \sqrt{(-2 - (-6))^2 + (2 - 5)^2} = \sqrt{(4)^2 + (-3)^2} = \sqrt{16 + 9} = \sqrt{25} = 5$$

Graphing Linear Inequalities

- To graph a linear inequality, first draw a graph of the "equals" line.

- Use a dash line for less than ($<$) and greater than ($>$) signs and a solid line for less than and equal to ($\leq$) and greater than and equal to ($\geq$).

- Choose a testing point. (it can be any point on both sides of the line.)

- Put the value of (x, y) of that point in the inequality. If that works, that part of the line is the solution. If the values don't work, then the other part of the line is the solution.

Example:

Sketch the graph of inequality: $y < 2x + 4$

Solution: To draw the graph of $y < 2x + 4$, you first need to graph the line:

$y = 2x + 4$

Since there is a less than ($<$) sign, draw a dash line.

The slope is 2 and y-intercept is 4.

Then, choose a testing point and substitute the value of x and y from that point into the inequality. The easiest point to test is the origin: $(0, 0)$

$$(0, 0) \rightarrow y < 2x + 4 \rightarrow 0 < 2(0) + 4 \rightarrow 0 < 4$$

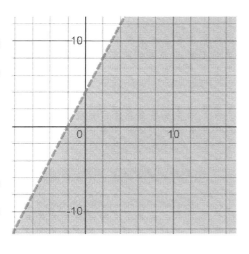

This is correct! 0 is less than 4. So, this part of the line (on the right side) is the solution of this inequality.

bit.ly/2S4IMr9

Find more at

Chapter 9: Practices

✍ Find the slope of each line.

1) $y = x - 5$

2) $y = 2x + 6$

3) $y = -5x - 8$

4) Line through $(2, 6)$ *and* $(5, 0)$

5) Line through $(8, 0)$ *and* $(-4, 3)$

6) Line through $(-2, -4)$ *and* $(-4, 8)$

✍ Sketch the graph of each line. (Using Slope−Intercept Form)

7) $y = x + 4$

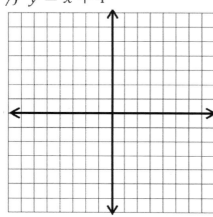

8) $y = 2x - 5$

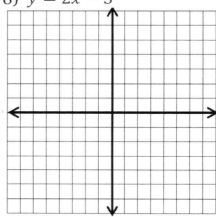

✍ Solve.

9) What is the equation of a line with slope 4 and intercept 16? _____

10) What is the equation of a line with slope 3 and passes through point $(1, 5)$?

_____

11) What is the equation of a line with slope -5 and passes through point $(-2, 7)$?

_____

12) The slope of a line is -4 and it passes through point $(-6, 2)$. What is the equation of the line? _____

13) The slope of a line is -3 and it passes through point $(-3, -6)$. What is the equation of the line? _____

✎ **Sketch the graph of each linear inequality.**

14) $y > 2x - 2$

15) $y < -x + 3$

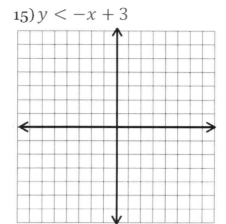

✎ **Find the midpoint of the line segment with the given endpoints.**

16) $(5, 0), (1, 4)$

17) $(2, 3), (4, 7)$

18) $(8, 1), (2, 5)$

19) $(5, 10), (3, 6)$

20) $(4, -1), (-2, 7)$

21) $(2, -5), (4, 1)$

22) $(7, 6), (-5, 2)$

23) $(-2, 8), (4, -6)$

✎ **Find the distance between each pair of points.**

24) $(-2, 8), (-6, 8)$

25) $(4, -4), (14, 20)$

26) $(-1, 9), (-5, 6)$

27) $(0, 3), (4, 3)$

28) $(0, -2), (5, 10)$

29) $(4, 3), (7, -1)$

30) $(2, 6), (10, -9)$

31) $(3, 3), (6, -1)$

32) $(-2, -12), (14, 18)$

33) $(2, -2), (12, 22)$

Effortless
Math
Education

Chapter 9: Answers

1) 1

2) 2

3) −5

4) −2

5) $-\frac{1}{4}$

6) −6

7) $y = x + 4$

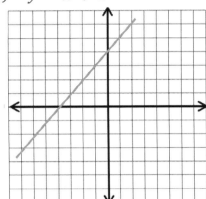

8) $y = 2x - 5$

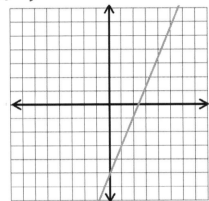

9) $y = 4x + 16$

10) $y = 3x + 2$

11) $y = -5x - 3$

12) $y = -4x - 22$

13) $y = -3x - 15$

14) $y > 2x - 2$

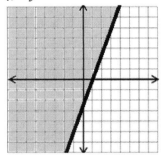

15) $y < -x + 3$

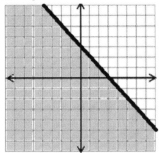

16) $(3, 2)$

17) $(3, 5)$

18) $(5, 3)$

19) $(4, 8)$

20) $(1, 3)$

21) $(3, -2)$

22) $(1, 4)$

23) $(1, 1)$

24) 4

25) 26

26) 5

27) 4

28) 13

29) 5

30) 17

31) 5

32) 34

33) 26

Effortless
Math
Education

CHAPTER

10 Polynomials

Math topics that you'll learn in this chapter:

- ☑ Simplifying Polynomials
- ☑ Adding and Subtracting Polynomials
- ☑ Multiplying Monomials
- ☑ Multiplying and Dividing Monomials
- ☑ Multiplying a Polynomial and a Monomial
- ☑ Multiplying Binomials
- ☑ Factoring Trinomials

Simplifying Polynomials

- To simplify Polynomials, find "like" terms. (they have same variables with same power).

- Use "FOIL". (First–Out–In–Last) for binomials:

$$(x + a)(x + b) = x^2 + (b + a)x + ab$$

- Add or Subtract "like" terms using order of operation.

Examples:

Example 1. Simplify this expression. $x(4x + 7) - 2x =$

Solution: Use Distributive Property: $x(4x + 7) = 4x^2 + 7x$
Now, combine like terms: $x(4x + 7) - 2x = 4x^2 + 7x - 2x = 4x^2 + 5x$

Example 2. Simplify this expression. $(x + 3)(x + 5) =$

Solution: First, apply the FOIL method: $(a + b)(c + d) = ac + ad + bc + bd$
$(x + 3)(x + 5) = x^2 + 5x + 3x + 15$
Now combine like terms: $x^2 + 5x + 3x + 15 = x^2 + 8x + 15$

Example 3. Simplify this expression. $2x(x - 5) - 3x^2 + 6x =$

Solution: Use Distributive Property: $2x(x - 5) = 2x^2 - 10x$
Then: $2x(x - 5) - 3x^2 + 6x = 2x^2 - 10x - 3x^2 + 6x$
Now combine like terms: $2x^2 - 3x^2 = -x^2$, and $-10x + 6x = -4x$
The simplified form of the expression: $2x^2 - 10x - 3x^2 + 6 = -x^2 - 4x$

Adding and Subtracting Polynomials

- Adding polynomials is just a matter of combining like terms, with some order of operations considerations thrown in.

- Be careful with the minus signs, and don't confuse addition and multiplication!

- For subtracting polynomials, sometimes you need to use the Distributive Property: $a(b + c) = ab + ac$, $a(b - c) = ab - ac$

Examples:

Example 1. Simplify the expressions. $(x^2 - 2x^3) - (x^3 - 3x^2) =$

Solution: First, use Distributive Property:
$$-(x^3 - 3x^2) = -x^3 + 3x^2$$
$\rightarrow (x^2 - 2x^3) - (x^3 - 3x^2) = x^2 - 2x^3 - x^3 + 3x^2$
Now combine like terms: $-2x^3 - x^3 = -3x^3$ and $x^2 + 3x^2 = 4x^2$
Then: $(x^2 - 2x^3) - (x^3 - 3x^2) = x^2 - 2x^3 - x^3 + 3x^2 = -3x^3 + 4x^2$

Example 2. Add expressions. $(3x^3 - 5) + (4x^3 - 2x^2) =$

Solution: Remove parentheses:
$(3x^3 - 5) + (4x^3 - 2x^2) = 3x^3 - 5 + 4x^3 - 2x^2$
Now combine like terms: $3x^3 - 5 + 4x^3 - 2x^2 = 7x^3 - 2x^2 - 5$

Example 3. Simplify the expressions. $(-4x^2 - 2x^3) - (5x^2 + 2x^3) =$

Solution: First, use Distributive Property:
$-(5x^2 + 2x^3) = -5x^2 - 2x^3 \rightarrow (-4x^2 - 2x^3) - (5x^2 + 2x^3)$
$$= -4x^2 - 2x^3 - 5x^2 - 2x^3$$
Now combine like terms and write in standard form:
$-4x^2 - 2x^3 - 5x^2 - 2x^3 = -4x^3 - 9x^2$

Multiplying Monomials

- A monomial is a polynomial with just one term: Examples: $2x$ or $7y^2$.

- When you multiply monomials, first multiply the coefficients (a number placed before and multiplying the variable) and then multiply the variables using multiplication property of exponents.

$$x^a \times x^b = x^{a+b}$$

Examples:

Example 1. Multiply expressions. $2xy^3 \times 6x^4y^2$

Solution: Find the same variables and use multiplication property of exponents: $x^a \times x^b = x^{a+b}$
$x \times x^4 = x^{1+4} = x^5$ and $y^3 \times y^2 = y^{3+2} = y^5$
Then, multiply coefficients and variables: $2xy^3 \times 6x^4y^2 = 12x^5y^5$

Example 2. Multiply expressions. $7a^3b^8 \times 3a^6b^4 =$

Solution: Use the multiplication property of exponents: $x^a \times x^b = x^{a+b}$
$a^3 \times a^6 = a^{3+6} = a^9$ and $b^8 \times b^4 = b^{8+4} = b^{12}$
Then: $7a^3b^8 \times 3a^6b^4 = 21a^9b^{12}$

Example 3. Multiply. $5x^2y^4z^3 \times 4x^4y^7z^5$

Solution: Use the multiplication property of exponents: $x^a \times x^b = x^{a+b}$
$x^2 \times x^4 = x^{2+4} = x^6$, $y^4 \times y^7 = y^{4+7} = y^{11}$ and $z^3 \times z^5 = z^{3+5} = z^8$
Then: $5x^2y^4z^3 \times 4x^4y^7z^5 = 20x^6y^{11}z^8$

Example 4. Simplify. $(-6a^7b^4)(4a^8b^5) =$

Solution: Use the multiplication property of exponents: $x^a \times x^b = x^{a+b}$
$a^7 \times a^8 = a^{7+8} = a^{15}$ and $b^4 \times b^5 = b^{4+5} = b^9$
Then: $(-6a^7b^4)(4a^8b^5) = -24a^{15}b^9$

Multiplying and Dividing Monomials

- When you divide or multiply two monomials, you need to divide or multiply their coefficients and then divide or multiply their variables.

- In case of exponents with the same base, for Division, subtract their powers, for Multiplication, add their powers.

- Exponent's Multiplication and Division rules:

$$x^a \times x^b = x^{a+b} \, , \qquad \frac{x^a}{x^b} = x^{a-b}$$

Examples:

Example 1. Multiply expressions. $(3x^5)(9x^4) =$

Solution: Use multiplication property of exponents:
$x^a \times x^b = x^{a+b} \rightarrow x^5 \times x^4 = x^9$
Then: $(3x^5)(9x^4) = 27x^9$

Example 2. Divide expressions. $\frac{12x^4y^6}{6xy^2} =$

Solution: Use division property of exponents:
$\frac{x^a}{x^b} = x^{a-b} \rightarrow \frac{x^4}{x} = x^{4-1} = x^3$ and $\frac{y^6}{y^2} = y^{6-2} = y^4$
Then: $\frac{12x^4y^6}{6xy^2} = 2x^3y^4$

Example 3. Divide expressions. $\frac{49a^6b^9}{7a^3b^4}$

Solution: Use division property of exponents:
$\frac{x^a}{x^b} = x^{a-b} \rightarrow \frac{a^6}{a^3} = a^{6-3} = a^3$ and $\frac{b^9}{b^4} = b^{9-4} = b^5$
Then: $\frac{49a^6b^9}{7a^3b^4} = 7a^3b^5$

Multiplying a Polynomial and a Monomial

- When multiplying monomials, use the product rule for exponents.

$$x^a \times x^b = x^{a+b}$$

- When multiplying a monomial by a polynomial, use the distributive property.

$$a \times (b + c) = a \times b + a \times c = ab + ac$$
$$a \times (b - c) = a \times b - a \times c = ab - ac$$

Examples:

Example 1. Multiply expressions. $6x(2x + 5)$

Solution: Use Distributive Property:
$6x(2x + 5) = 6x \times 2x + 6x \times 5 = 12x^2 + 30x$

Example 2. Multiply expressions. $x(3x^2 + 4y^2)$

Solution: Use Distributive Property:
$x(3x^2 + 4y^2) = x \times 3x^2 + x \times 4y^2 = 3x^3 + 4xy^2$

Example 3. Multiply. $-x(-2x^2 + 4x + 5)$

Solution: Use Distributive Property:
$-x(-2x^2 + 4x + 5) = (-x)(-2x^2) + (-x) \times (4x) + (-x) \times (5) =$
Now simplify:
$(-x)(-2x^2) + (-x) \times (4x) + (-x) \times (5) = 2x^3 - 4x^2 - 5x$

Multiplying Binomials

- A binomial is a polynomial that is the sum or the difference of two terms, each of which is a monomial.

- To multiply two binomials, use the "FOIL" method. (First–Out–In–Last)

$$(x + a)(x + b) = x \times x + x \times b + a \times x + a \times b = x^2 + bx + ax + ab$$

Examples:

Example 1. Multiply Binomials. $(x + 3)(x - 2) =$

Solution: Use "FOIL". (First–Out–In–Last):
$(x + 3)(x - 2) = x^2 - 2x + 3x - 6$
Then combine like terms: $x^2 - 2x + 3x - 6 = x^2 + x - 6$

Example 2. Multiply. $(x + 6)(x + 4) =$

Solution: Use "FOIL". (First–Out–In–Last):
$(x + 6)(x + 4) = x^2 + 4x + 6x + 24$
Then simplify: $x^2 + 4x + 6x + 24 = x^2 + 10x + 24$

Example 3. Multiply. $(x + 5)(x - 7) =$

Solution: Use "FOIL". (First–Out–In–Last):
$(x + 5)(x - 7) = x^2 - 7x + 5x - 35$
Then simplify: $x^2 - 7x + 5x - 35 = x^2 - 2x - 35$

Example 4. Multiply Binomials. $(x - 9)(x - 5) =$

Solution: Use "FOIL". (First–Out–In–Last):
$(x - 9)(x - 5) = x^2 - 5x - 9x + 45$
Then combine like terms: $x^2 - 5x - 9x + 45 = x^2 - 14x + 45$

bit.ly/3aCs0FL
Find more at

Factoring Trinomials

To factor trinomials, you can use following methods:

- "FOIL": $(x + a)(x + b) = x^2 + (b + a)x + ab$

- "Difference of Squares":

$$a^2 - b^2 = (a + b)(a - b)$$
$$a^2 + 2ab + b^2 = (a + b)(a + b)$$
$$a^2 - 2ab + b^2 = (a - b)(a - b)$$

- "Reverse FOIL": $x^2 + (b + a)x + ab = (x + a)(x + b)$

Examples:

Example 1. Factor this trinomial. $x^2 - 2x - 8$

Solution: Break the expression into groups. You need to find two numbers that their product is -8 and their sum is -2. (remember "Reverse FOIL": $x^2 + (b + a)x + ab = (x + a)(x + b)$). Those two numbers are 2 and -4. Then: $x^2 - 2x - 8 = (x^2 + 2x) + (-4x - 8)$
Now factor out x from $x^2 + 2x$: $x(x + 2)$, and factor out -4 from $-4x - 8$: $-4(x + 2)$; Then: $(x^2 + 2x) + (-4x - 8) = x(x + 2) - 4(x + 2)$
Now factor out like term: $(x + 2)$. Then: $(x + 2)(x - 4)$

Example 2. Factor this trinomial. $x^2 - 2x - 24$

Solution: Break the expression into groups: $(x^2 + 4x) + (-6x - 24)$
Now factor out x from $x^2 + 4x$: $x(x + 4)$, and factor out -6 from $-6x - 24$: $-6(x + 4)$; Then: $(x + 4) - 6(x + 4)$, now factor out like term: $(x + 4) \rightarrow x(x + 4) - 6(x + 4) = (x + 4)(x - 6)$

Find more at
bit.ly/38EpdJA

EffortlessMath.com

Chapter 10: Practices

✍ Simplify each polynomial.

1) $3(6x + 4) =$

2) $5(3x - 8) =$

3) $x(7x + 2) + 9x =$

4) $6x(x + 3) + 5x =$

5) $6x(3x + 1) - 5x =$

6) $x(3x - 4) + 3x^2 - 6 =$

7) $x^2 - 5 - 3x(x + 8) =$

8) $2x^2 + 7 - 6x(2x + 5) =$

✍ Add or subtract polynomials.

9) $(x^2 + 3) + (2x^2 - 4) =$

10) $(3x^2 - 6x) - (x^2 + 8x) =$

11) $(4x^3 - 3x^2) + (2x^3 - 5x^2) =$

12) $(6x^3 - 7x) - (5x^3 - 3x) =$

13) $(10x^3 + 4x^2) + (14x^2 - 8) =$

14) $(4x^3 - 9) - (3x^3 - 7x^2) =$

15) $(9x^3 + 3x) - (6x^3 - 4x) =$

16) $(7x^3 - 5x) - (3x^3 + 5x) =$

✍ Find the products. (Multiplying Monomials)

17) $3x^2 \times 8x^3 =$

18) $2x^4 \times 9x^3 =$

19) $-4a^4b \times 2ab^3 =$

20) $(-7x^3yz) \times (3xy^2z^4) =$

21) $-2a^5bc \times 6a^2b^4 =$

22) $9u^3t^2 \times (-2ut) =$

23) $12x^2z \times 3xy^3 =$

24) $11x^3z \times 5xy^5 =$

25) $-6a^3bc \times 5a^4b^3 =$

26) $-4x^6y^2 \times (-12xy) =$

Effortless Math Education

✎ **Simplify each expression. (Multiplying and Dividing Monomials)**

27) $(7x^2y^3)(3x^4y^2) =$

28) $(6x^3y^2)(4x^4y^3) =$

29) $(10x^8y^5)(3x^5y^7) =$

30) $(15a^3b^2)(2a^3b^8) =$

31) $\dfrac{42x^4y^2}{6x^3y} =$

32) $\dfrac{49x^5y^6}{7x^2y} =$

33) $\dfrac{63x^{15}y^{10}}{9x^8y^6} =$

34) $\dfrac{35x^8y^{12}}{5x^4y^8} =$

✎ **Find each product. (Multiplying a Polynomial and a Monomial)**

35) $3x(5x - y) =$

36) $2x(4x + y) =$

37) $7x(x - 3y) =$

38) $x(2x^2 + 2x - 4) =$

39) $5x(3x^2 + 8x + 2) =$

40) $7x(2x^2 - 9x - 5) =$

✎ **Find each product. (Multiplying Binomials)**

41) $(x - 3)(x + 3) =$

42) $(x - 6)(x + 6) =$

43) $(x + 10)(x + 4) =$

44) $(x - 6)(x + 7) =$

45) $(x + 2)(x - 5) =$

46) $(x - 10)(x + 3) =$

✎ **Factor each trinomial.**

47) $x^2 + 6x + 8 =$

48) $x^2 + 3x - 10 =$

49) $x^2 + 2x - 48 =$

50) $x^2 - 10x + 16 =$

51) $2x^2 - 10x + 12 =$

52) $3x^2 - 10x + 3 =$

Effortless
Math
Education

Effortless
Math
Education

Chapter 10: Answers

1) $18x + 12$

2) $15x - 40$

3) $7x^2 + 11x$

4) $6x^2 + 23x$

5) $18x^2 + x$

6) $6x^2 - 4x - 6$

7) $-2x^2 - 24x - 5$

8) $-10x^2 - 30x + 7$

9) $3x^2 - 1$

10) $2x^2 - 14x$

11) $6x^3 - 8x^2$

12) $x^3 - 4x$

13) $10x^3 + 18x^2 - 8$

14) $x^3 + 7x^2 - 9$

15) $3x^3 + 7x$

16) $4x^3 - 10x$

17) $24x^5$

18) $18x^7$

19) $-8a^5b^4$

20) $-21x^4y^3z^5$

21) $-12a^7b^5c$

22) $-18u^4t^3$

23) $36x^3y^3z$

24) $55x^4y^5z$

25) $-30a^7b^4c$

26) $48x^7y^3$

27) $21x^6y^5$

28) $24x^7y^5$

29) $30x^{13}y^{12}$

30) $30a^6b^{10}$

31) $7xy$

32) $7x^3y^5$

33) $7x^7y^4$

34) $7x^4y^4$

35) $15x^2 - 3xy$

36) $8x^2 + 2xy$

37) $7x^2 - 21xy$

38) $2x^3 + 2x^2 - 4x$

39) $15x^3 + 40x^2 + 10x$

40) $14x^3 - 63x^2 - 35x$

41) $x^2 - 9$

42) $x^2 - 36$

43) $x^2 + 14x + 40$

44) $x^2 + x - 42$

45) $x^2 - 3x - 10$

46) $x^2 - 7x - 30$

47) $(x + 4)(x + 2)$

48) $(x + 5)(x - 2)$

49) $(x - 6)(x + 8)$

50) $(x - 8)(x - 2)$

51) $(2x - 4)(x - 3)$

52) $(3x - 1)(x - 3)$

**Effortless
Math
Education**

CHAPTER

11 Geometry and Solid Figures

Math topics that you'll learn in this chapter:

- ☑ The Pythagorean Theorem
- ☑ Complementary and Supplementary angles
- ☑ Parallel lines and Transversals
- ☑ Triangles
- ☑ Special Right Triangles
- ☑ Polygons
- ☑ Circles
- ☑ Trapezoids
- ☑ Cubes
- ☑ Rectangle Prisms
- ☑ Cylinder

99

The Pythagorean Theorem

- You can use the Pythagorean Theorem to find a missing side in a right triangle.

- In any right triangle: $a^2 + b^2 = c^2$

Examples:

Example 1. Right triangle ABC (not shown) has two legs of lengths 3 cm (AB) and 4 cm (AC). What is the length of the hypotenuse of the triangle (side BC)?

Solution: Use Pythagorean Theorem: $a^2 + b^2 = c^2$, $a = 3$, and $b = 4$

Then: $a^2 + b^2 = c^2 \rightarrow 3^2 + 4^2 = c^2 \rightarrow 9 + 16 = c^2 \rightarrow 25 = c^2 \rightarrow c = \sqrt{25} = 5$

The length of the hypotenuse is 5 cm.

Example 2. Find the hypotenuse of this triangle.

Solution: Use Pythagorean Theorem: $a^2 + b^2 = c^2$

Then: $a^2 + b^2 = c^2 \rightarrow 8^2 + 6^2 = c^2 \rightarrow 64 + 36 = c^2$

$c^2 = 100 \rightarrow c = \sqrt{100} = 10$

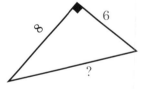

Example 3. Find the length of the missing side in this triangle.

Solution: Use Pythagorean Theorem: $a^2 + b^2 = c^2$

Then: $a^2 + b^2 = c^2 \rightarrow 12^2 + b^2 = 15^2 \rightarrow 144 + b^2 = 225 \rightarrow$

$b^2 = 225 - 144 \rightarrow b^2 = 81 \rightarrow b = \sqrt{81} = 9$

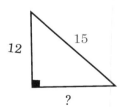

Complementary and Supplementary angles

- Two angles with a sum of 90 degrees are called complementary angles.

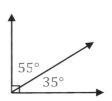

- Two angles with a sum of 180 degrees are Supplementary angles.

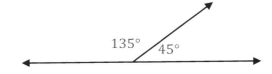

Examples:

Example 1. Find the missing angle.

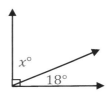

Solution: Notice that the two angles form a right angle. This means that the angles are complementary, and their sum is 90.

Then: $18 + x = 90 \rightarrow x = 90^\circ - 18^\circ = 72^\circ$

The missing angle is 72 degrees. $x = 72^\circ$

Example 2. Angles Q and S are supplementary. What is the measure of angle Q if angle S is 35 degrees?

Solution: Q and S are supplementary $\rightarrow Q + S = 180 \rightarrow Q + 35 = 180 \rightarrow$

$$Q = 180 - 35 = 145$$

Parallel lines and Transversals

- When a line (transversal) intersects two parallel lines in the same plane, eight angles are formed. In the following diagram, a transversal intersects two parallel lines. Angles 1, 3, 5, and 7 are congruent. Angles 2, 4, 6, and 8 are also congruent.

- In the following diagram, the following angles are supplementary angles (their sum is 180):

    ❖ Angles 1 and 8

    ❖ Angles 2 and 7

    ❖ Angles 3 and 6

    ❖ Angles 4 and 5

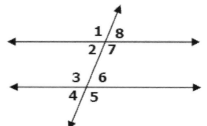

Example:

In the following diagram, two parallel lines are cut by a transversal. What is the value of x?

Solution: The two angles $3x - 15$ and $2x + 7$ are equivalent.

That is: $3x - 15 = 2x + 7$

Now, solve for x:

$3x - 15 + 15 = 2x + 7 + 15$

$\rightarrow 3x = 2x + 22 \rightarrow 3x - 2x = 2x + 22 - 2x$

$\rightarrow x = 22$

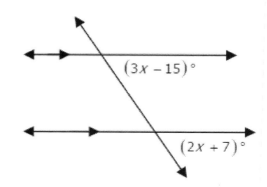

Triangles

- In any triangle, the sum of all angles is 180 degrees.
- Area of a triangle $= \frac{1}{2} (base \times height)$

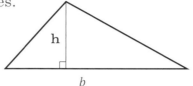

Examples:

What is the area of the following triangles?

Example 1.

Solution: Use the area formula:
Area $= \frac{1}{2} (base \times height)$
$base = 14$ and $height = 10$
Area $= \frac{1}{2}(14 \times 10) = \frac{1}{2}(140) = 70$

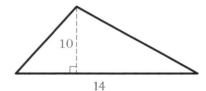

Example 2.

Solution: Use the area formula:
Area $= \frac{1}{2} (base \times height)$
$base = 16$ and $height = 8$; Area $= \frac{1}{2}(16 \times 8) = \frac{128}{2} = 64$

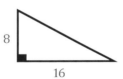

Example 3. What is the missing angle in this triangle?

Solution:
In any triangle, the sum of all angles is 180 degrees.
Let x be the missing angle.
Then: $55 + 80 + x = 180$;
$\rightarrow 135 + x = 180 \rightarrow x = 180 - 135 = 45$
The missing angle is 45 degrees.

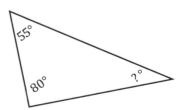

bit.ly/3haZrRg
Find more at

Special Right Triangles

- A special right triangle is a triangle whose sides are in a particular ratio. Two special right triangles are $45° - 45° - 90°$ and $30° - 60° - 90°$ triangles.

- In a special $45° - 45° - 90°$ triangle, the three angles are $45°$, $45°$ and $90°$. The lengths of the sides of this triangle are in the ratio of $1:1:\sqrt{2}$.

- In a special triangle $30° - 60° - 90°$, the three angles are $30° - 60° - 90°$. The lengths of this triangle are in the ratio of $1:\sqrt{3}:2$.

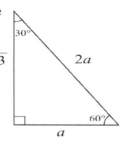

Examples:

Example 1. Find the length of the hypotenuse of a right triangle if the length of the other two sides are both 4 inches.

Solution: this is a right triangle with two equal sides. Therefore, it must be a $45° - 45° - 90°$ triangle. Two equivalent sides are 4 inches. The ratio of sides: $x: x: x\sqrt{2}$
The length of the hypotenuse is $4\sqrt{2}$ inches. $x: x: x\sqrt{2} \rightarrow 4: 4: 4\sqrt{2}$

Example 2. The length of the hypotenuse of a triangle is 6 inches. What are the lengths of the other two sides if one angle of the triangle is $30°$?

Solution: The hypotenuse is 6 inches and the triangle is a $30° - 60° - 90°$ triangle.
Then, one side of the triangle is 3 (it's half the side of the hypotenuse) and the other side is $3\sqrt{3}$. (it's the smallest side times $\sqrt{3}$)
$x: x\sqrt{3}: 2x \rightarrow x = 3 \rightarrow x: x\sqrt{3}: 2x = 3: 3\sqrt{3}: 6$

Polygons

- The perimeter of a square = $4 \times side = 4s$

- The perimeter of a rectangle= $2(width + length)$

- The perimeter of trapezoid= $a + b + c + d$

- The perimeter of a regular hexagon = $6a$

- The perimeter of a parallelogram = $2(l + w)$

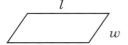

Examples:

Example 1. Find the perimeter of following regular hexagon.

Solution: Since the hexagon is regular, all sides are equal.
Then: The perimeter of The hexagon = $6 \times (one\ side)$
The perimeter of The hexagon = $6 \times (one\ side) = 6 \times 8 = 48\ m$

Example 2. Find the perimeter of following trapezoid.

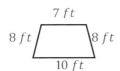

Solution: The perimeter of a trapezoid = $a + b + c + d$
The perimeter of the trapezoid = $7 + 8 + 8 + 10 = 33\ ft$

Circles

- In a circle, variable r is usually used for the radius and d for diameter.

- *Area of a circle* $= \pi r^2$ (π is about 3.14)

- *Circumference of a circle* $= 2\pi r$

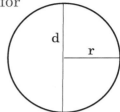

Examples:

Example 1. Find the area of this circle.

Solution:
Use area formula: $Area = \pi r^2$
$r = 6 \, in \rightarrow Area = \pi(6)^2 = 36\pi$, $\pi = 3.14$
Then: $Area = 36 \times 3.14 = 113.04 \, in^2$

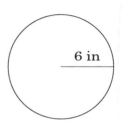

Example 2. Find the Circumference of this circle.

Solution:
Use Circumference formula: $Circumference = 2\pi r$
$r = 8 \, cm \rightarrow Circumference = 2\pi(8) = 16\pi$
$\pi = 3.14$ Then: $Circumference = 16 \times 3.14 = 50.24 \, cm$

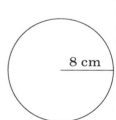

Example 3. Find the area of the circle.

Solution:
Use area formula: $Area = \pi r^2$,
$r = 9 \, in$ then: $Area = \pi(9)^2 = 81\pi$, $\pi = 3.14$
Then: $Area = 81 \times 3.14 = 254.34 \, in^2$

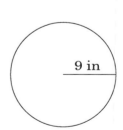

Trapezoids

- A quadrilateral with at least one pair of parallel sides is a trapezoid.

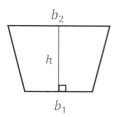

- Area of a trapezoid $= \frac{1}{2}h(b_1 + b_2)$

Examples:

Example 1. Calculate the area of this trapezoid.

Solution:

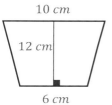

Use area formula: A $= \frac{1}{2}h(b_1 + b_2)$

$b_1 = 6\ cm$, $b_2 = 10\ cm$ and $h = 12\ cm$

Then: A $= \frac{1}{2}(12)(10 + 6) = 6(16) = 96\ cm^2$

Example 2. Calculate the area of this trapezoid.

Solution:

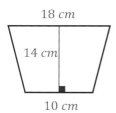

Use area formula: A $= \frac{1}{2}h(b_1 + b_2)$

$b_1 = 10\ cm$, $b_2 = 18\ cm$ and $h = 14\ cm$

Then: A $= \frac{1}{2}(14)(10 + 18) = 7(28) = 196\ cm^2$

Cubes

- A cube is a three-dimensional solid object bounded by six square sides.

- Volume is the measure of the amount of space inside of a solid figure, like a cube, ball, cylinder or pyramid.

- The volume of a cube = $(one\ side)^3$

- The surface area of a cube = $6 \times (one\ side)^2$

Examples:

Example 1. Find the volume and surface area of this cube.

Solution: Use volume formula: $volume = (one\ side)^3$
Then: $volume = (one\ side)^3 = (3)^3 = 27\ cm^3$
Use surface area formula:
$surface\ area\ of\ cube$: $6(one\ side)^2 = 6(3)^2 = 6(9) = 54\ cm^2$

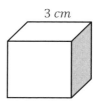
3 cm

Example 2. Find the volume and surface area of this cube.

Solution: Use volume formula: $volume = (one\ side)^3$
Then: $volume = (one\ side)^3 = (6)^3 = 216\ cm^3$
Use surface area formula:
$surface\ area\ of\ cube$: $6(one\ side)^2 = 6(6)^2 = 6(36) = 216\ cm^2$

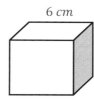
6 cm

Example 3. Find the volume and surface area of this cube.

Solution: Use volume formula: $volume = (one\ side)^3$
Then: $volume = (one\ side)^3 = (8)^3 = 512\ m^3$
Use surface area formula:
$surface\ area\ of\ cube$: $6(one\ side)^2 = 6(8)^2 = 6(64) = 384\ m^2$

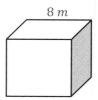
8 m

Rectangular Prisms

- A rectangular prism is a solid 3-dimensional object with six rectangular faces.

- The volume of a Rectangular prism $= Length \times Width \times Height$

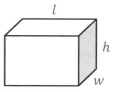

$Volume = l \times w \times h$

$Surface\ area = 2 \times (wh + lw + lh)$

Examples:

Example 1. Find the volume and surface area of this rectangular prism.

Solution: Use volume formula: $Volume = l \times w \times h$

Then: $Volume = 7 \times 5 \times 9 = 315\ m^3$

Use surface area formula: $Surface\ area = 2 \times (wh + lw + lh)$

Then: $Surface\ area = 2 \times \big((5 \times 9) + (7 \times 5) + (7 \times 9)\big)$

$\qquad\qquad = 2 \times (45 + 35 + 63) = 2 \times (143) = 286\ m^2$

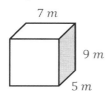

Example 2. Find the volume and surface area of this rectangular prism.

Solution: Use volume formula: $Volume = l \times w \times h$

Then: $Volume = 9 \times 6 \times 12 = 648\ m^3$

Use surface area formula: $Surface\ area = 2 \times (wh + lw + lh)$

Then: $Surface\ area = 2 \times \big((6 \times 12) + (9 \times 6) + (9 \times 12)\big)$

$\qquad\qquad = 2 \times (72 + 54 + 108) = 2 \times (234) = 468\ m^2$

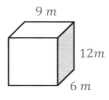

bit.ly/3nKm2G

Find more at

Cylinder

- A cylinder is a solid geometric figure with straight parallel sides and a circular or oval cross-section.

- *Volume of a Cylinder* $= \pi(radius)^2 \times height$, $\pi \approx 3.14$

- *Surface area of a cylinder* $= 2\pi r^2 + 2\pi rh$

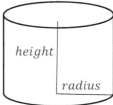

Examples:

Example 1. Find the volume and Surface area of the follow Cylinder.

Solution: Use volume formula:

$Volume = \pi(radius)^2 \times height$

Then: $Volume = \pi(4)^2 \times 10 = 16\pi \times 10 = 160\pi$

$\pi = 3.14$ then: $Volume = 160\pi = 160 \times 3.14 = 502.4\ cm^3$

Use surface area formula: $Surface\ area = 2\pi r^2 + 2\pi rh$

Then: $2\pi(4)^2 + 2\pi(4)(10) = 2\pi(16) + 2\pi(40) = 32\pi + 80\pi = 112\pi$

$\pi = 3.14$ Then: $Surface\ area = 112 \times 3.14 = 351.68\ cm^2$

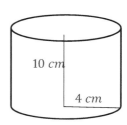

Example 2. Find the volume and Surface area of the follow Cylinder.

Solution: Use volume formula:

$Volume = \pi(radius)^2 \times height$

Then: $Volume = \pi(5)^2 \times 8 = \pi 25 \times 8 = 200\pi$

$\pi = 3.14$ then: $Volume = 200\pi = 628\ cm^3$

Use surface area formula: $Surface\ area = 2\pi r^2 + 2\pi rh$

Then: $= 2\pi(5)^2 + 2\pi(5)(8) = 2\pi(25) + 2\pi(40) = 50\pi + 80\pi = 130\pi$

$\pi = 3.14$ then: $Surface\ area = 130 \times 3.14 = 408.2\ cm^2$

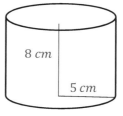

Chapter 11: Practices

✎ Find the missing side?

1)　　　2)　　　3)　　　4)

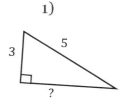
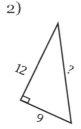
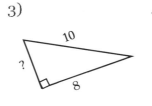
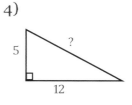

✎ Find the measure of the unknown angle in each triangle.

5)　　　6)　　　7)　　　8)

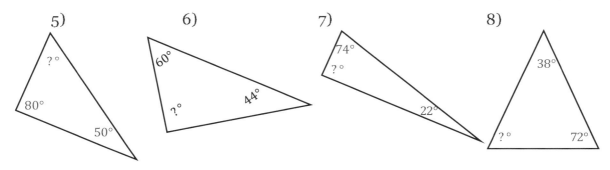

✎ Find the area of each triangle.

9)　　　10)　　　11)　　　12)

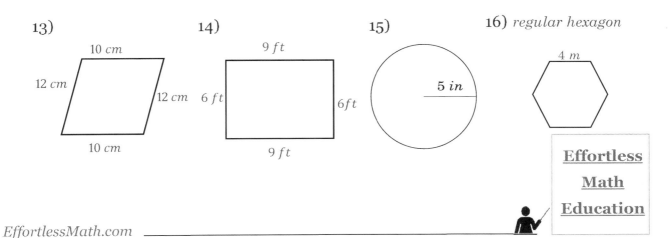

✎ Find the perimeter or circumference of each shape.

13)　　　14)　　　15)　　　16) *regular hexagon*

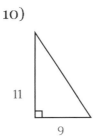
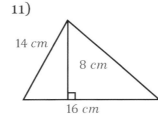
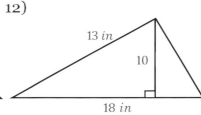

**Effortless
Math
Education**

✍ **Find the area of each trapezoid.**

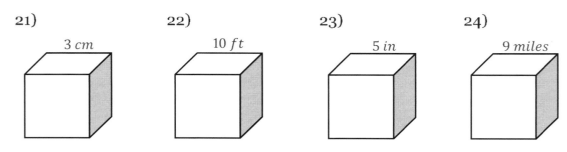

17) 10 m 7 m 14 m

18) 10 cm 8 cm 15 cm

19) 8 ft 6 ft 13 ft

20) 8 cm 6 cm 12 cm

✍ **Find the volume of each cube.**

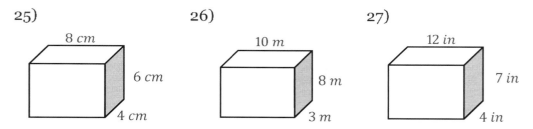

21) 3 cm

22) 10 ft

23) 5 in

24) 9 miles

✍ **Find the volume of each Rectangular Prism.**

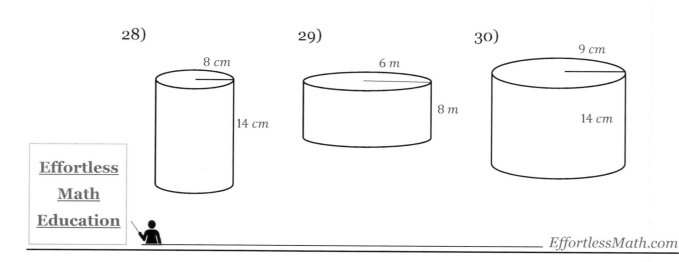

25) 8 cm 6 cm 4 cm

26) 10 m 8 m 3 m

27) 12 in 7 in 4 in

✍ **Find the volume of each Cylinder. Round your answer to the nearest tenth. ($\pi = 3.14$)**

28) 8 cm 14 cm

29) 6 m 8 m

30) 9 cm 14 cm

Effortless
Math
Education

Chapter 11: Answers

1)   4

2)   15

3)   6

4)   13

5)   50

6)   76

7)   84

8)   70

9)   30

10) 49.5

11) $64 \; cm^2$

12) $90 \; in^2$

13) $44 \; cm$

14) $30 \; ft$

15) $10 \, \pi \approx 31.4 \; in$

16) $24 \; m$

17) $84 \; m^2$

18) $100 \; cm^2$

19) $63 \; ft^2$

20) $60 \; cm^2$

21) $27 \; cm^3$

22) $1,000 \; ft^3$

23) $125 \; in^3$

24) $729 \; mi^3$

25) $192 \; cm^3$

26) $240 \; m^3$

27) $336 \; in^3$

28) $2,813.44 \; cm^3$

29) $904.32 \; m^3$

30) $3,560.76 \; cm^3$

Effortless
Math
Education

CHAPTER

12 Statistics

Math topics that you'll learn in this chapter:

- ☑ Mean, Median, Mode, and Range of the Given Data
- ☑ Pie Graph
- ☑ Probability Problems
- ☑ Permutations and Combinations

115

Mean, Median, Mode, and Range of the Given Data

- Mean: $\dfrac{\textit{sum of the data}}{\textit{total number of data entires}}$

- Mode: the value in the list that appears most often

- Median: is the middle number of a group of numbers arranged in order by size.

- Range: the difference of the largest value and smallest value in the list

Examples:

Example 1. What is the mode of these numbers? $5, 6, 8, 6, 8, 5, 3, 5$

Solution: Mode: the value in the list that appears most often.
Therefore, the mode is number 5. There are three number 5 in the data.

Example 2. What is the median of these numbers? $6, 11, 15, 10, 17, 20, 7$

Solution: Write the numbers in order: $6, 7, 10, 11, 15, 17, 20$
The median is the number in the middle. Therefore, the median is 11.

Example 3. What is the mean of these numbers? $7, 2, 3, 2, 4, 8, 7, 5$

Solution: Mean: $\dfrac{\textit{sum of the data}}{\textit{total number of data entires}} = \dfrac{7+2+3+2+4+8+7+5}{8} = \dfrac{38}{8} = 4.75$

Example 4. What is the range in this list? $3, 7, 12, 6, 15, 20, 8$

Solution: Range is the difference of the largest value and smallest value in the list. The largest value is 20 and the smallest value is 3.
Then: $20 - 3 = 17$

Find more at bit.ly/2KO86gg

Pie Graph

- A Pie Chart is a circle chart divided into sectors, each sector represents the relative size of each value.

- Pie charts represent a snapshot of how a group is broken down into smaller pieces.

Examples:

A library has 750 books that include Mathematics, Physics, Chemistry, English and History. Use the following graph to answer the questions.

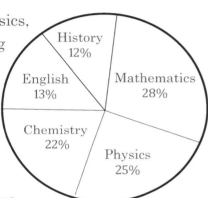

Example 1. What is the number of Mathematics books?

Solution: Number of total books = 750
Percent of Mathematics books = 28% = 0.28
Then, the number of Mathematics books: 0.28 × 750 = 210

Example 2. What is the number of History books?

Solution: Number of total books = 750
Percent of History books = 12% = 0.12
Then: 0.12 × 750 = 90

Example 3. What is the number of Chemistry books?

Solution: Number of total books = 750
Percent of Chemistry books = 22% = 0.22
Then: 0.22 × 750 = 165

bit.ly/34ECTDv

Find more at

Probability Problems

- Probability is the likelihood of something happening in the future. It is expressed as a number between zero (can never happen) to 1 (will always happen).

- Probability can be expressed as a fraction, a decimal, or a percent.

- Probability formula: $Probability = \frac{number\ of\ desired\ outcomes}{number\ of\ total\ outcomes}$

Examples:

Example 1. Anita's trick–or–treat bag contains 10 pieces of chocolate, 16 suckers, 16 pieces of gum, 22 pieces of licorice. If she randomly pulls a piece of candy from her bag, what is the probability of her pulling out a piece of sucker?

Solution: $Probability = \frac{number\ of\ desired\ outcomes}{number\ of\ total\ outcomes}$

Probability of pulling out a piece of sucker $= \frac{16}{10+16+16+22} = \frac{16}{64} = \frac{1}{4}$

Example 2. A bag contains 20 balls: four green, five black, eight blue, a brown, a red and one white. If 19 balls are removed from the bag at random, what is the probability that a brown ball has been removed?

Solution: If 19 balls are removed from the bag at random, there will be one ball in the bag. The probability of choosing a brown ball is 1 out of 20. Therefore, the probability of not choosing a brown ball is 19 out of 20 and the probability of having not a brown ball after removing 19 balls is the same. The answer is: $\frac{19}{20}$

Permutations and Combinations

Factorials are products, indicated by an exclamation mark. For example, $4! = 4 \times 3 \times 2 \times 1$ (Remember that $0!$ is defined to be equal to 1)

- **Permutations:** The number of ways to choose a sample of k elements from a set of n distinct objects where order does matter, and replacements are not allowed. For a permutation problem, use this formula:

$$_nP_k = \frac{n!}{(n-k)!}$$

- **Combination:** The number of ways to choose a sample of r elements from a set of n distinct objects where order does not matter, and replacements are not allowed. For a combination problem, use this formula:

$$_nC_r = \frac{n!}{r!\,(n-r)!}$$

Examples:

Example 1. How many ways can the first and second place be awarded to 7 people?

Solution: Since the order matters, (the first and second place are different!) we need to use permutation formula where n is 7 and k is 2. Then: $\frac{n!}{(n-k)!} = \frac{7!}{(7-2)!} = \frac{7!}{5!} = \frac{7 \times 6 \times 5!}{5!}$, remove $5!$ from both sides of the fraction. Then: $\frac{7 \times 6 \times 5!}{5!} = 7 \times 6 = 42$

Example 2. How many ways can we pick a team of 3 people from a group of 8?

Solution: Since the order doesn't matter, we need to use a combination formula where n is 8 and r is 3.
Then: $\frac{n!}{r!\,(n-r)!} = \frac{8!}{3!\,(8-3)!} = \frac{8!}{3!\,(5)!} = \frac{8 \times 7 \times 6 \times 5!}{3!\,(5)!} = \frac{8 \times 7 \times 6}{3 \times 2 \times 1} = \frac{336}{6} = 56$

Chapter 12: Practices

✍ Find the values of the Given Data.

1) $6, 11, 5, 3, 6$

Mode: _____   Range: _____

Mean: _____   Median: _____

2) $4, 9, 1, 9, 6, 7$

Mode: _____   Range: _____

Mean: _____   Median: _____

3) $10, 3, 6, 10, 4, 15$

Mode: _____   Range: _____

Mean: _____   Median: _____

4) $12, 4, 8, 9, 3, 12, 15$

Mode: _____   Range: _____

Mean: _____   Median: _____

✍ The circle graph below shows all Bob's expenses for last month. Bob spent $790 on his Rent last month.

5) How much did Bob's total expenses last month? _____

6) How much did Bob spend for foods last month? _____

7) How much did Bob spend for his bills last month? _____

8) How much did Bob spend on his car last month? _____

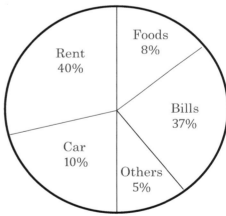

Bob's last month expenses

Rent 40%
Foods 8%
Bills 37%
Others 5%
Car 10%

Effortless Math Education

🖊 **Solve.**

9) Bag A contains 8 red marbles and 6 green marbles. Bag B contains 5 black marbles and 7 orange marbles. What is the probability of selecting a green marble at random from bag A? What is the probability of selecting a black marble at random from Bag B?

_____   _____

🖊 **Solve.**

10) Susan is baking cookies. She uses sugar, flour, butter, and eggs. How many different orders of ingredients can she try? _____

11) Jason is planning for his vacation. He wants to go to museum, go to the beach, and play volleyball. How many different ways of ordering are there for him? _____

12) In how many ways can a team of 6 basketball players choose a captain and co-captain? _____

13) How many ways can you give 5 balls to your 8 friends? _____

14) A professor is going to arrange her 5 students in a straight line. In how many ways can she do this? _____

15) In how many ways can a teacher chooses 12 out of 15 students? _____

Effortless
Math
Education

Chapter 12: Answers

1) Mode: 6, Range: 8, Mean: 6.2, Median: 6

2) Mode: 9, Range:8, Mean: 6, Median: 6.5

3) Mode: 10, Range: 12, Mean: 8, Median: 8

4) Mode: 12, Range: 12, Mean: 9, Median: 9

5) $1,975

6) $158

7) $730.75

8) $197.50

9) $\frac{3}{7}, \frac{5}{12}$

10) 24

11) 6

12) 30 (it's a permutation problem)

13) 56 (it's a combination problem)

14) 120

15) 455 (it's a combination problem)

13 Functions Operations

Math topics that you'll learn in this chapter:

- ☑ Function Notation and Evaluation
- ☑ Adding and Subtracting Functions
- ☑ Multiplying and Dividing Functions
- ☑ Composition of Functions
- ☑ Function Inverses

123

Function Notation and Evaluation

- Functions are mathematical operations that assign unique outputs to given inputs.

- Function notation is the way a function is written. It is meant to be a precise way of giving information about the function without a rather lengthy written explanation.

- The most popular function notation is $f(x)$ which is read "f of x". Any letter can name a function. for example: $g(x)$, $h(x)$, etc.

- To evaluate a function, plug in the input (the given value or expression) for the function's variable (place holder, x).

Examples:

Example 1. Evaluate: $f(x) = x + 6$, find $f(2)$

Solution: Substitute x with 2:
Then: $f(x) = x + 6 \rightarrow f(2) = 2 + 6 \rightarrow f(2) = 8$

Example 2. Evaluate: $w(x) = 3x - 1$, find $w(4)$.

Solution: Substitute x with 4:
Then: $w(x) = 3x - 1 \rightarrow w(4) = 3(4) - 1 = 12 - 1 = 11$

Example 3. Evaluate: $f(x) = 2x^2 + 4$, find $f(-1)$.

Solution: Substitute x with -1:
Then: $f(x) = 2x^2 + 4 \rightarrow f(-1) = 2(-1)^2 + 4 \rightarrow f(-1) = 2 + 4 = 6$

Example 4. Evaluate: $h(x) = 4x^2 - 9$, find $h(2a)$.

Solution: Substitute x with $3a$:
Then: $h(x) = 4x^2 - 9 \rightarrow h(2a) = 4(2a)^2 - 9 \rightarrow h(2a) = 4(4a^2) - 9 = 16a^2 - 9$

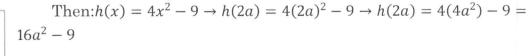

Adding and Subtracting Functions

- Just like we can add and subtract numbers and expressions, we can add or subtract two functions and simplify or evaluate them. The result is a new function.

- For two functions $f(x)$ and $g(x)$, we can create two new functions:

$$(f + g)(x) = f(x) + g(x) \text{ and } (f - g)(x) = f(x) - g(x)$$

Examples:

Example 1. $g(x) = 2x - 2$, $f(x) = x + 1$, Find: $(g + f)(x)$

Solution: $(g + f)(x) = g(x) + f(x)$
Then: $(g + f)(x) = (2x - 2) + (x + 1) = 2x - 2 + x + 1 = 3x - 1$

Example 2. $f(x) = 4x - 3$, $g(x) = 2x - 4$, Find: $(f - g)(x)$

Solution: $(f - g)(x) = f(x) - g(x)$
Then: $(f - g)(x) = (4x - 3) - (2x - 4) = 4x - 3 - 2x + 4 = 2x + 1$

Example 3. $g(x) = x^2 + 2$, $f(x) = x + 5$, Find: $(g + f)(x)$

Solution: $(g + f)(x) = g(x) + f(x)$
Then: $(g + f)(x) = (x^2 + 2) + (x + 5) = x^2 + x + 7$

Example 4. $f(x) = 5x^2 - 3$, $g(x) = 3x + 6$, Find: $(f - g)(3)$

Solution: $(f - g)(x) = f(x) - g(x)$
Then: $(f - g)(x) = (5x^2 - 3) - (3x + 6) = 5x^2 - 3 - 3x - 6 = 5x^2 - 3x - 9$
Substitute x with 3: $(f - g)(3) = 5(3)^2 - 3(3) - 9 = 45 - 9 - 9 = 27$

bit.ly/3hdeFVO

Find more at

Multiplying and Dividing Functions

- Just like we can multiply and divide numbers and expressions, we can multiply and divide two functions and simplify or evaluate them.

- For two functions $f(x)$ and $g(x)$, we can create two new functions:

$$(f.g)(x) = f(x).g(x) \quad \text{and} \quad \left(\frac{f}{g}\right)(x) = \frac{f(x)}{g(x)}$$

Examples:

Example 1. $g(x) = x + 3$, $f(x) = x + 4$, Find: $(g.f)(x)$

Solution:

$$(g.f)(x) = g(x).f(x) = (x + 3)(x + 4) = x^2 + 4x + 3x + 12 = x^2 + 7x + 12$$

Example 2. $f(x) = x + 6$, $h(x) = x - 9$, Find: $\left(\frac{f}{h}\right)(x)$

Solution: $\left(\frac{f}{h}\right)(x) = \frac{f(x)}{h(x)} = \frac{x+6}{x-9}$

Example 3. $g(x) = x + 7$, $f(x) = x - 3$, Find: $(g.f)(2)$

Solution: $(g.f)(x) = g(x).f(x) = (x + 7)(x - 3) = x^2 - 3x + 7x - 21 \quad g(x).f(x) = x^2 + 4x - 21$

Substitute x with 2: $(g.f)(x) = (2)^2 + 4(2) - 21 = 4 + 8 - 21 = -9$

Example 4. $f(x) = x + 3$, $h(x) = 2x - 4$, Find: $\left(\frac{f}{h}\right)(3)$

Solution: $\left(\frac{f}{h}\right)(x) = \frac{f(x)}{h(x)} = \frac{x+3}{2x-4}$

Substitute x with 3: $\left(\frac{f}{h}\right)(x) = \frac{x+3}{2x-4} = \frac{3+3}{2(3)-4} = \frac{6}{2} = 3$

Composition of Functions

- "Composition of functions" simply means combining two or more functions in a way where the output from one function becomes the input for the next function.

- The notation used for composition is: $(fog)(x) = f\big(g(x)\big)$ and is read "f composed with g of x" or "f of g of x".

Examples:

Example 1. Using $f(x) = 2x + 3$ and $g(x) = 5x$, find: $(fog)(x)$

Solution: $(fog)(x) = f\big(g(x)\big)$. Then: $(fog)(x) = f\big(g(x)\big) = f(5x)$
Now find $f(5x)$ by substituting x with $5x$ in $f(x)$ function.
Then: $f(x) = 2x + 3$; $(x \to 5x) \to f(5x) = 2(5x) + 3 = 10x + 3$

Example 2. Using $f(x) = 3x - 1$ and $g(x) = 2x - 2$, find: $(gof)(5)$

Solution: $(fog)(x) = f\big(g(x)\big)$. Then: $(gof)(x) = g\big(f(x)\big) = g(3x - 1)$,
Now substitute x in $g(x)$ by $(3x - 1)$.
Then: $g(3x - 1) = 2(3x - 1) - 2 = 6x - 2 - 2 = 6x - 4$
Substitute x with 5: $(gof)(5) = g\big(f(x)\big) = 6x - 4 = 6(5) - 4 = 26$

Example 3. Using $f(x) = 2x^2 - 5$ and $g(x) = x + 3$, find: $f\big(g(3)\big)$

Solution: First, find $g(3)$: $g(x) = x + 3 \to g(3) = 3 + 3 = 6$
Then: $f\big(g(3)\big) = f(6)$. Now, find $f(6)$ by substituting x with 6 in $f(x)$ function.
$f\big(g(3)\big) = f(6) = 2(6)^2 - 5 = 2(36) - 5 = 67$

bit.ly/2WHBkAg

Find more at

Function Inverses

- An inverse function is a function that reverses another function: if the function f applied to an input x gives a result of y, then applying its inverse function g to y gives the result x. $f(x) = y$ if and only if $g(y) = x$

- The inverse function of $f(x)$ is usually shown by $f^{-1}(x)$.

Examples:

Example 1. Find the inverse of the function: $f(x) = 2x - 1$

Solution: First, replace $f(x)$ with y: $y = 2x - 1$, Then, replace all $x's$ with y and all $y's$ with x: $x = 2y - 1$, Now, solve for y: $x = 2y - 1 \rightarrow x + 1 = 2y \rightarrow \frac{1}{2}x + \frac{1}{2} = y$ Finally replace y with $f^{-1}(x)$: $f^{-1}(x) = \frac{1}{2}x + \frac{1}{2}$

Example 2. Find the inverse of the function: $g(x) = \frac{1}{5}x + 3$

Solution: $g(x) = \frac{1}{5}x + 3 \rightarrow y = \frac{1}{5}x + 3 \rightarrow$ replace all $x's$ with y and all $y's$ with x

$x = \frac{1}{5}y + 3$, solve for y: $\rightarrow x - 3 = \frac{1}{5}y \rightarrow 5(x - 3) = y \rightarrow y = 5x - 15 \rightarrow$

$$g^{-1}(x) = 5x - 15$$

Example 3. Find the inverse of the function: $h(x) = \sqrt{x} + 6$

Solution: $h(x) = \sqrt{x} + 6 \rightarrow y = \sqrt{x} + 6$, replace all $x's$ with y and all $y's$ with x

$\rightarrow x = \sqrt{y} + 6 \rightarrow x - 6 = \sqrt{y} \rightarrow (x - 6)^2 = (\sqrt{y})^2 \rightarrow x^2 - 12x + 36 = y$

$\rightarrow h^{-1}(x) = x^2 - 12x + 36$

Chapter 13: Practices

✍ Evaluate each function.

1) $g(n) = 2n + 5$, find $g(2)$

_____

2) $h(x) = 5x - 9$, find $h(4)$

_____

3) $k(n) = 10 - 6n$, find $k(2)$

_____

4) $g(x) = -5x + 6$, find $g(-2)$

_____

5) $k(n) = -8n + 3$, find $k(-6)$

_____

6) $w(n) = -2n - 9$, find $w(-5)$

_____

✍ Perform the indicated operation.

7) $f(x) = x + 6$
   $g(x) = 3x + 2$
   Find $(f - g)(x)$

_____

8) $g(x) = x - 9$
   $f(x) = 2x - 1$
   Find $(g - f)(x)$

_____

9) $h(t) = 5t + 6$
   $g(t) = 2t + 4$
   Find $(h + g)(x)$

_____

10) $g(a) = -6a + 1$
    $f(a) = 3a^2 - 3$
    Find $(g + f)(5)$

_____

11) $g(x) = 7x - 1$
    $h(x) = -4x^2 + 2$
    Find $(g - h)(-3)$

_____

12) $h(x) = -x^2 - 1$
    $g(x) = -7x - 1$
    Find $(h - g)(-5)$

_____

Effortless
Math
Education

✒ Perform the indicated operation.

13) $g(x) = x + 3$

$f(x) = x + 1$

Find $(g.f)(x)$

_____

14) $f(x) = 4x$

$h(x) = x - 6$

Find $(f.h)(x)$

_____

15) $g(a) = a - 8$

$h(a) = 4a - 2$

Find $(g.h)(3)$

_____

16) $f(x) = 6x + 2$

$h(x) = 5x - 1$

Find $\left(\frac{f}{h}\right)(-2)$

_____

17) $f(x) = 7a - 1$

$g(x) = -5 - 2a$

Find $\left(\frac{f}{g}\right)(-4)$

_____

18) $g(a) = a^2 - 4$

$f(a) = a + 6$

Find $\left(\frac{g}{f}\right)(-3)$

_____

✒ Using $f(x) = 4x + 3$ and $g(x) = x - 7$, find:

19) $g\big(f(2)\big) =$_____

20) $g\big(f(-2)\big) =$_____

21) $f\big(g(4)\big) =$_____

22) $f\big(f(7)\big) =$_____

23) $g\big(f(5)\big) =$_____

24) $g\big(f(-5)\big) =$_____

✒ Find the inverse of each function.

25) $f(x) = \frac{1}{x} - 6 \rightarrow f^{-1}(x) =$

26) $g(x) = \frac{7}{-x-3} \rightarrow g^{-1}(x) =$

27) $h(x) = \frac{x+9}{3} \rightarrow h^{-1}(x) =$

28) $h(x) = \frac{2x-10}{4} \rightarrow h^{-1}(x) =$

29) $f(x) = \frac{-15+x}{3} \rightarrow f^{-1}(x) =$

30) $s(x) = \sqrt{x} - 2 \rightarrow s^{-1}(x) =$

Effortless

Math

Education

Effortless
Math
Education

Chapter 13: Answers

1)   9

2)   11

3) -2

4)   16

5)   51

6)   1

7) $-2x + 4$

8) $-x - 8$

9) $7t + 10$

10)   43

11)   12

12) -60

13) $x^2 + 4x + 3$

14) $4x^2 - 24x$

15) -50

16) $\frac{10}{11}$

17) $-\frac{29}{3}$

18) $\frac{5}{3}$

19)   4

20) -12

21) -9

22)   127

23)   16

24) -24

25) $f^{-1}(x) = \frac{1}{x+6}$

26) $g^{-1}(x) = -\frac{7+3x}{x}$

27) $h^{-1}(x) = 3x - 9$

28) $h^{-1}(x) = 2x + 5$

29) $f^{-1}(x) = 3x + 15$

30) $s^{-1}(x) = x^2 + 4x + 4$

CHAPTER

14 Quadratic

Math topics that you'll learn in this chapter:

- ☑ Solving a Quadratic Equation
- ☑ Graphing Quadratic Functions
- ☑ Solving Quadratic Inequalities
- ☑ Graphing Quadratic Inequalities

133

Solving a Quadratic Equation

- Write the equation in the form of: $ax^2 + bx + c = 0$

- Factorize the quadratic, set each factor equal to zero and solve.

- Use quadratic formula if you couldn't factorize the quadratic.

- Quadratic formula: $x = \frac{-b \pm \sqrt{b^2 - 4ac}}{2a}$

Examples:

Find the solutions of each quadratic function.

Example 1. $x^2 + 7x + 12 = 0$

Solution: Factor the quadratic by grouping. We need to find two numbers whose sum is 7 (from $7x$) and whose product is 12. Those numbers are 3 and 4. Then: $x^2 + 7x + 12 = 0 \rightarrow x^2 + 3x + 4x + 12 = 0 \rightarrow (x^2 + 3x) + (4x + 12) = 0$, Now, find common factors: $(x^2 + 3x) = x(x + 3)$ and $(4x + 12) = 3(x + 4)$. We have two expressions $(x^2 + 3x)$ and $(4x + 12)$ and their common factor is $(x + 3)$. Then: $(x^2 + 3x) + (4x + 12) = 0 \rightarrow x(x + 3) + 4(x + 3) = 0 \rightarrow (x + 3)(x + 4) = 0$.
The product of two expressions is 0. Then:
$(x + 3) = 0 \rightarrow x = -3$ or $(x + 4) = 0 \rightarrow x = -4$

Example 2. $x^2 + 5x + 6 = 0$

Solution: Use quadratic formula: $x_{1,2} = \frac{-b \pm \sqrt{b^2 - 4ac}}{2a}$, $a = 1, b = 5$ and $c = 6$

Then: $x = \frac{-5 \pm \sqrt{5^2 - 4 \times 1(6)}}{2(1)}$, $x_1 = \frac{-5 + \sqrt{5^2 - 4 \times 1(6)}}{2(1)} = -2$, $x_2 = \frac{-5 - \sqrt{5^2 - 4 \times 1(6)}}{2(1)} = -3$

Graphing Quadratic Functions

- Quadratic functions in vertex form: $y = a(x - h)^2 + k$ where (h, k) is the vertex of the function. The axis of symmetry is $x = h$

- Quadratic functions in standard form: $y = ax^2 + bx + c$ where $x = -\frac{b}{2a}$ is the value of x in the vertex of the function.

- To graph a quadratic function, first find the vertex, then substitute some values for x and solve for y. (Remember that the graph of a quadratic function is a U-shaped curve and it is called "parabola".)

Example:

Sketch the graph of $y = (x + 2)^2 - 3$

Solution: Quadratic functions in vertex form: $y = a(x - h)^2 + k$ and (h, k) is the vertex. Then, the vertex of $y = (x + 2)^2 - 3$ is $(-2, -3)$.

Substitute zero for x and solve for y:
$y = (0 + 2)^2 - 3 = 1$.
The y Intercept is $(0, 1)$.

Now, you can simply graph the quadratic function. Notice that quadratic function is a U-shaped curve.

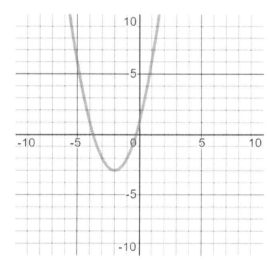

Solving Quadratic Inequalities

- A quadratic inequality is one that can be written in the standard form of

$ax^2 + bx + c > 0$ (or substitute $<, \leq$, or $\geq$ for $>$).

- Solving a quadratic inequality is like solving equations. We need to find the solutions (the zeroes).

- To solve quadratic inequalities, first find quadratic equations. Then choose a test value between zeroes. Finally, find interval(s), such as > 0 or < 0.

Examples:

Example 1. Solve quadratic inequality. $x^2 + x - 6 > 0$

Solution: First solve $x^2 + x - 6 = 0$ by factoring. Then: $x^2 + x - 6 = 0 \rightarrow (x-2)(x+3) = 0$. The product of two expressions is 0. Then: $(x-2) = 0 \rightarrow x = 2$ or $(x+3) = 0 \rightarrow x = -3$. Now, choose a value between 2 and -3. Let's choose 0. Then: $x = 0 \rightarrow x^2 + x - 6 > 0 \rightarrow (0)^2 + (0) - 6 > 0 \rightarrow -6 > 0$

-6 is not greater than 0. Therefore, all values between 2 and -3 are NOT the solution of this quadratic inequality. The solution is: $x > 2$ and $x < -3$. To represent the solution, we can use interval notation, in which solution sets are indicated with parentheses or brackets. The solutions $x > 2$ and $x < -3$ represented as: $(\infty, -3) \cup (2, \infty)$

Solution $x \geq 2$ represented as: $[2, \infty)$

Example 2. Solve quadratic inequality. $x^2 - 2x - 8 \geq 0$

Solution: First solve: $x^2 - 2x - 8 = 0$, Factor: $x^2 - 2x - 8 = 0 \rightarrow (x-4)(x+2) = 0$.

-2 and 4 are the solutions. Choose a point between -2 and 4. Let's choose 0.

Then: $x = 0 \rightarrow x^2 - 2x - 8 \geq 0 \rightarrow (0)^2 - 2(0) - 8 \geq 0 \rightarrow -8 \geq 0$.

This is NOT true. So, the solution is: $x \leq -2$ or $x \geq 4$ (using interval notation the solution is: $(\infty, -2] \cup [4, \infty)$

Graphing Quadratic Inequalities

- A quadratic inequality is in the form

  $y > ax^2 + bx + c$ (or substitute $<, \leq,$ or $\geq$ for $>$).

- To graph a quadratic inequality, start by graphing the quadratic parabola. Then fill in the region either inside or outside of it, depending on the inequality.

- Choose a testing point and check the solution section.

Example:

Sketch the graph of $y > 2x^2$

Solution: First, graph the quadratic $y = 2x^2$ Since the inequality sing is $>$, we need to use dash lines.

Now, choose a testing point inside the parabola. Let's choose $(0,2)$.

$y > 2x^2 \rightarrow 2 > 2(0)^2 \rightarrow 2 > 0$

This is true. So, inside the parabola is the solution section.

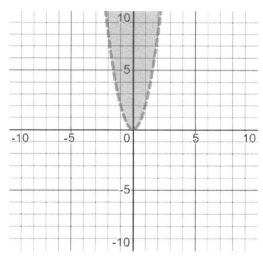

Chapter 14: Practices

✎ **Solve each equation by factoring or using the quadratic formula.**

1) $x^2 - 4x - 32 = 0$

_____

2) $x^2 - 2x - 63 = 0$

_____

3) $x^2 + 17x + 72 = 0$

_____

4) $x^2 + 14x + 48 = 0$

_____

5) $x^2 + 5x - 24 = 0$

_____

6) $x^2 + 15x + 36 = 0$

_____

✎ **Sketch the graph of each function.**

7) $y = (x + 1)^2 - 2$

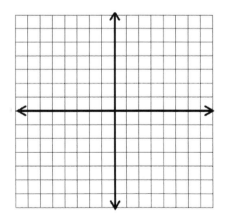

8) $y = (x - 1)^2 + 3$

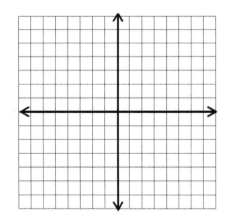

✎ **Solve each quadratic inequality.**

9) $x^2 - 4 < 0$

_____

10) $x^2 - 9 > 0$

_____

11) $x^2 - 5x - 6 < 0$

_____

12) $x^2 + 8x - 20 > 0$

_____

13) $x^2 + 10x - 24 \geq 0$

_____

14) $x^2 + 17x + 72 \leq 0$

_____

✎ **Sketch the graph of each quadratic inequality.**

15) $y < -2x^2$

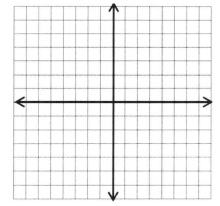

16) $y > 3x^2$

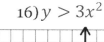

Effortless
Math
Education

Chapter 14: Answers

1) $x^2 - 4x - 32 = 0$

   $x = 8, x = -4$

2) $x^2 - 2x - 63 = 0$

   $x = 9, x = -7$

3) $x^2 + 17x + 72 = 0$

   $x = -9, x = -8$

4) $x^2 + 14x + 48 = 0$

   $x = -6, x = -8$

5) $x^2 + 5x - 24 = 0$

   $x = 3, x = -8$

6) $x^2 + 15x + 36 = 0$

   $x = -12, x = -3$

7) $y = (x + 1)^2 - 2$

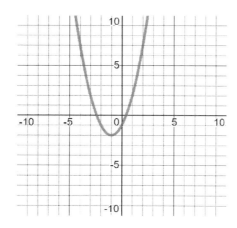

8) $y = (x - 1)^2 + 3$

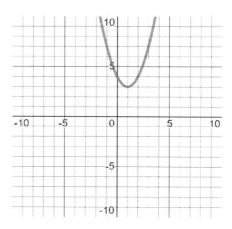

9) $x^2 - 4 < 0$

   $-2 < x < 2$

10) $x^2 - 9 > 0$

   $-3 < x < 3$

11) $x^2 - 5x - 6 < 0$

   $-1 < x < 6$

12) $x^2 + 8x - 20 > 0$

   $x < -10 \ or \ x > 2$

13) $x^2 + 10x - 24 \geq 0$

   $x \leq -12 \ or \ x \geq 2$

14) $x^2 + 17x + 72 \leq 0$

   $-9 \leq x \leq -8$

Effortless
Math
Education

15) $y < -2x^2$

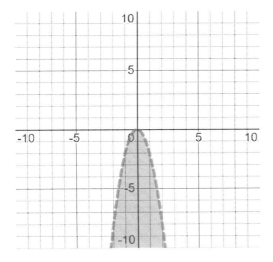

16) $y > 3x^2$

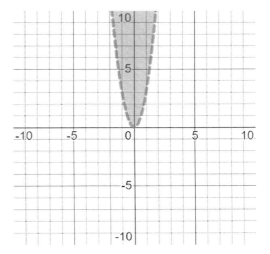

Effortless Math Education

15 Complex Numbers

Math topics that you'll learn in this chapter:

☑ Adding and Subtracting Complex Numbers

☑ Multiplying and Dividing Complex Numbers

☑ Rationalizing Imaginary Denominators

143

Adding and Subtracting Complex Numbers

- A complex number is expressed in the form $a + bi$, where a and b are real numbers, and i, which is called an imaginary number, is a solution of the equation $x^2 = -1$

- For adding complex numbers:

$$(a + bi) + (c + di) = (a + c) + (b + d)i$$

- For subtracting complex numbers:

$$(a + bi) - (c + di) = (a - c) + (b - d)i$$

Examples:

Example 1. Solve: $(8 + 4i) + (6 - 2i)$

Solution: Remove parentheses: $(8 + 4i) + (6 - 2i) = 8 + 4i + 6 - 2i$
Combine like terms: $8 + 4i + 6 - 2i = 14 + 2i$

Example 2. Solve: $(10 + 8i) + (8 - 3i)$

Solution: Remove parentheses: $(10 + 8i) + (8 - 3i) = 10 + 8i + 8 - 3i$
Group like terms: $10 + 8i + 8 - 3i = 18 + 5i$

Example 3. Solve: $(-5 - 3i) - (2 + 4i)$

Solution: Remove parentheses by multiplying -1 to the second parentheses:
$$(-5 - 3i) - (2 + 4i) = -5 - 3i - 2 - 4i$$
Combine like terms: $-5 - 3i - 2 - 4i = -7 - 7i$

Multiplying and Dividing Complex Numbers

- You can use FOIL (First-Out-In-Last) method or the following rule to multiply imaginary numbers. Remember that: $i^2 = -1$

$$(a + bi) + (c + di) = (ac - bd) + (ad + bc)i$$

- To divide complex numbers, you need to find the conjugate of the denominator. Conjugate of $(a + bi)$ is $(a - bi)$.

- Dividing complex numbers: $\frac{a+bi}{c+di} = \frac{a+bi}{c+di} \times \frac{c-di}{c-di} = \frac{ac+bd}{c^2+d^2} + \frac{bc-ad}{c^2+d^2}i$

Examples:

Example 1. Solve: $\frac{6-2i}{2+i}$

Solution: The conjugate of $(2 + i)$ is $(2 - i)$. Use the rule for dividing complex numbers:

$$\frac{a + bi}{c + di} = \frac{a + bi}{c + di} \times \frac{c - di}{c - di} = \frac{ac + bd}{c^2 + d^2} + \frac{bc - ad}{c^2 + d^2}i \rightarrow$$

$$\frac{6 - 2i}{2 + i} \times \frac{2 - i}{2 - i} = \frac{6 \times (2) + (-2)(1)}{2^2 + (1)^2} + \frac{-2 \times 2 - (6)(1)}{2^2 + (1)^2}i = \frac{10}{5} + \frac{-10}{5}i = 2 - 2i$$

Example 2. Solve: $(2 - 3i)(6 - 3i)$

Solution: Use the multiplication of imaginary numbers rule:

$$(a + bi) + (c + di) = (ac - bd) + (ad + bc)i$$
$$\left(2 \times 6 - (-3)(-3)\right) + (2(-3) + (-3) \times 6)i = 3 - 24i$$

Example 3. Solve: $\frac{3-2i}{4+i}$

Solution: Use the rule for dividing complex numbers: $\frac{a+bi}{c+di} = \frac{a+bi}{c+di} \times \frac{c-di}{c-di} =$

$\frac{ac+bd}{c^2+d^2} + \frac{bc-ad}{c^2+d^2}i \rightarrow \frac{3-2i}{4+i} \times \frac{4-i}{4-i} = \frac{(3\times4+(-2)\times1)+(-2\times4-3\times1)i}{4^2+1^2} = \frac{10-11i}{17} =$
$\frac{10}{17} - \frac{11}{17}i$

Rationalizing Imaginary Denominators

- Step 1: Find the conjugate (it's the denominator with different sign between the two terms).

- Step 2: Multiply numerator and denominator by the conjugate.

- Step 3: Simplify if needed.

Examples:

Example 1. Solve: $\frac{4-3i}{6i}$

Solution: Multiply both numerator and denominator by $\frac{i}{i}$:

$$\frac{4-3i}{6i} = \frac{(4-3i)(i)}{6i(i)} = \frac{(4)(i)-(3i)(i)}{6(i^2)} = \frac{4i-3i^2}{6(-1)} = \frac{4i-3(-1)}{-6} = \frac{4i}{-6} + \frac{3}{-6} = -\frac{1}{2} - \frac{2}{3}i$$

Example 2. Solve: $\frac{6i}{2-i}$

Solution: Multiply both numerator and denominator by the conjugate

$\frac{2+i}{2+i}$: $\frac{6i(2+i)}{(2-i)(2+i)}$ = Apply complex arithmetic rule: $(a+bi)(a-bi) = a^2 + b^2$

$2^2 + (-1)^2 = 5$, then: $\frac{6i(2+i)}{(2-i)(2+i)} = \frac{-6+12i}{5} = -\frac{6}{5} + \frac{12}{5}i$

Example 3. Solve: $\frac{8-2i}{2i}$

Solution: Factor 2 from both sides: $\frac{8-2i}{2i} = \frac{2(4-i)}{2i}$, divide both sides by 2:

$\frac{2(4-i)}{2i} = \frac{(4-i)}{i}$

Multiply both numerator and denominator by $\frac{i}{i}$:

$$\frac{(4-i)}{i} = \frac{(4-i)}{i} \times \frac{i}{i} = \frac{(4i-i^2)}{i^2} = \frac{1+4i}{-1} = -1 - 4i$$

bit.ly/3vC5eoO

Find more at

Chapter 15: Practices

✎ Evaluate.

1) $(-5i) - (7i) =$

2) $(-2i) + (-8i) =$

3) $(2i) - (6 + 3i) =$

4) $(4 - 6i) + (-2i) =$

5) $(-7i) + (4 + 5i) =$

6) $10 + (-2 - 6i) =$

7) $(-3i) - (9 + 2i) =$

8) $(4 + 6i) - (-3i) =$

✎ Calculate.

9) $(3 - 2i)(4 - 3i) =$

10) $(6 + 2i)(3 + 2i) =$

11) $(8 - i)(4 - 2i) =$

12) $(2 - 4i)(3 - 5i) =$

13) $(5 + 6i)(3 + 2i) =$

14) $(5 + 3i)(9 + 2i) =$

✎ Simplify.

15) $\frac{3}{2i} =$

16) $\frac{8}{-3i} =$

17) $\frac{-9}{2i} =$

18) $\frac{2-3i}{-5i} =$

19) $\frac{4-5i}{-2i} =$

20) $\frac{8+3i}{2i} =$

Effortless
Math
Education

Answers – Chapter 15

1) $-12i$

2) $-10i$

3) $-6 - i$

4) $4 - 8i$

5) $4 - 2i$

6) $8 - 6i$

7) $-9 - 5i$

8) $4 + 9i$

9) $6 - 17i$

10) $14 + 18i$

11) $30 - 20i$

12) $-14 - 22i$

13) $3 + 28i$

14) $39 + 37i$

15) $-\dfrac{3i}{2}$

16) $\dfrac{8i}{3}$

17) $-\dfrac{9i}{2}$

18) $\dfrac{3}{5} + \dfrac{2}{5}i$

19) $\dfrac{5}{2} + 2i$

20) $\dfrac{3}{2} - 4i$

CHAPTER

16 Radicals

Math topics that you'll learn in this chapter:

☑ Simplifying Radical Expressions

☑ Adding and Subtracting Radical Expressions

☑ Multiplying Radical Expressions

☑ Rationalizing Radical Expressions

☑ Radical Equations

☑ Domain and Range of Radical Functions

149

Simplifying Radical Expressions

- Find the prime factors of the numbers or expressions inside the radical.

- Use radical properties to simplify the radical expression:

$$\sqrt[n]{x^a} = x^{\frac{a}{n}}, \sqrt[n]{xy} = x^{\frac{1}{n}} \times y^{\frac{1}{n}}, \sqrt[n]{\frac{x}{y}} = \frac{x^{\frac{1}{n}}}{y^{\frac{1}{n}}}, \text{ and } \sqrt[n]{x} \times \sqrt[n]{y} = \sqrt[n]{xy}$$

Examples:

Example 1. Find the square root of $\sqrt{144x^2}$.

Solution: Find the factor of the expression $144x^2$: $144 = 12 \times 12$ and $x^2 = x \times x$, now use radical rule: $\sqrt[n]{a^n} = a$, Then: $\sqrt{12^2} = 12$ and $\sqrt{x^2} = x$
Finally: $\sqrt{144x^2} = \sqrt{12^2} \times \sqrt{x^2} = 12 \times x = 12x$

Example 2. Write this radical in exponential form. $\sqrt[3]{x^4}$

Solution: To write a radical in exponential form, use this rule: $\sqrt[n]{x^a} = x^{\frac{a}{n}}$
Then: $\sqrt[3]{x^4} = x^{\frac{4}{3}}$

Example 3. Simplify. $\sqrt{8x^3}$

Solution: First factor the expression $8x^3$: $8x^3 = 2^3 \times x \times x \times x$, we need to find perfect squares: $8x^3 = 2^2 \times 2 \times x^2 \times x = 2^2 \times x^2 \times 2x$,
Then: $\sqrt{8x^3} = \sqrt{2^2 \times x^2} \times \sqrt{2x}$
Now use radical rule: $\sqrt[n]{a^n} = a$, Then: $\sqrt{2^2 \times x^2} \times \sqrt{(2x)} = 2x \times \sqrt{2x} = 2x\sqrt{2x}$

Example 4. Simplify. $\sqrt{27a^5b^4}$

Solution: First factor the expression $27a^5b^4$: $27a^5b^4 = 3^3 \times a^5 \times b^4$, we need to find perfect squares: $27a^5b^4 = 3^2 \times 3 \times a^4 \times a \times b^4$, Then:
$$\sqrt{27a^5b^4} = \sqrt{3^2 \times a^4 \times b^4} \times \sqrt{3a}$$
Now use radical rule: $\sqrt[n]{a^n} = a$, Then:
$$\sqrt{3^2 \times a^4 \times b^4} \times \sqrt{3a} = 3 \times a^2 \times b^2 \times \sqrt{3a} = 3a^2b^2\sqrt{3a}$$

Adding and Subtracting Radical Expressions

- Only numbers and expressions that have the same radical part can be added or subtracted.

- Remember, combining "unlike" radical terms is not possible.

- For numbers with the same radical part, just add or subtract factors outside the radicals.

Examples:

Example 1. Simplify: $8\sqrt{2} + 4\sqrt{2}$

Solution: Since we have the same radical parts, then we can add these two radicals: Add like terms: $8\sqrt{2} + 4\sqrt{2} = 12\sqrt{2}$

Example 2. Simplify: $11\sqrt{7} + 6\sqrt{7}$

Solution: Since we have the same radical parts, then we can add these two radicals: Add like terms: $11\sqrt{7} + 6\sqrt{7} = 17\sqrt{7}$

Example 3. Simplify: $2\sqrt{8} - 2\sqrt{2}$

Solution: The two radical parts are not the same. First, we need to simplify the $2\sqrt{8}$. Then: $2\sqrt{8} = 2\sqrt{4 \times 2} = 2(\sqrt{4})(\sqrt{2}) = 4\sqrt{2}$
Now, combine like terms: $2\sqrt{8} - 2\sqrt{2} = 4\sqrt{2} - 2\sqrt{2} = 2\sqrt{2}$

Example 4. Simplify: $5\sqrt{27} + 3\sqrt{3}$

Solution: The two radical parts are not the same. First, we need to simplify the $5\sqrt{27}$. Then: $5\sqrt{27} = 5\sqrt{9 \times 3} = 5(\sqrt{9})(\sqrt{3}) = 15\sqrt{3}$
Now, add: $5\sqrt{27} + 3\sqrt{3} = 15\sqrt{3} + 3\sqrt{3} = 18\sqrt{3}$

bit.ly/2PkJfTA
Find more at

Multiplying Radical Expressions

To multiply radical expressions:

- Multiply the numbers and expressions outside of the radicals.

- Multiply the numbers and expressions inside the radicals.

- Simplify if needed.

Examples:

Example 1. Evaluate. $2\sqrt{5} \times \sqrt{3}$

Solution: Multiply the numbers outside of the radicals and the radical parts.
Then: $2\sqrt{5} \times \sqrt{3} = 2 \times 1 \times \sqrt{5} \times \sqrt{3} = 2\sqrt{15}$

Example 2. Multiply. $3x\sqrt{3} \times 4\sqrt{x}$

Solution: Multiply the numbers outside of the radicals and the radical parts.
Then, simplify: $3x\sqrt{3} \times 4\sqrt{x} = (3x \times 4) \times (\sqrt{3} \times \sqrt{x}) = (12x)(\sqrt{3x}) = 12x\sqrt{3x}$

Example 3. Evaluate. $5a\sqrt{5b} \times \sqrt{2b}$

Solution: Multiply the numbers outside of the radicals and the radical parts.
Then: $5a\sqrt{5b} \times \sqrt{2b} = 5a \times 1 \times \sqrt{5b} \times \sqrt{2b} = 5a\sqrt{10b^2}$
Simplify: $5a\sqrt{10b^2} = 5a \times \sqrt{10} \times \sqrt{b^2} = 5ab\sqrt{10}$

Example 4. Simplify. $11\sqrt{2x} \times 2\sqrt{8x}$

Solution: Multiply the numbers outside of the radicals and the radical parts.
Then, simplify: $11\sqrt{2x} \times 2\sqrt{8x} = (11 \times 2) \times (\sqrt{2x} \times \sqrt{8x}) = (22)(\sqrt{16x^2}) = 22\sqrt{16x^2}$
$\sqrt{16x^2} = 4x$, then: $22\sqrt{16x^2} = 22 \times 4x = 88x$

Rationalizing Radical Expressions

- Radical expressions cannot be in the denominator. (number in the bottom)

- To get rid of the radical in the denominator, multiply both numerator and denominator by the radical in the denominator.

- If there is a radical and another integer in the denominator, multiply both numerator and denominator by the conjugate of the denominator.

- The conjugate of $(a + b)$ is $(a - b)$ and vice versa.

Examples:

Example 1. Simplify $\frac{6}{\sqrt{2}}$

Solution: Multiply both numerator and denominator by $\sqrt{2}$. Then:

$\frac{6}{\sqrt{2}} \times \frac{\sqrt{2}}{\sqrt{2}} = \frac{6\sqrt{2}}{\sqrt{4}} = \frac{6\sqrt{2}}{2}$, Now, simplify: $\frac{6\sqrt{2}}{2} = 3\sqrt{2}$

Example 2. Simplify $\frac{5}{\sqrt{6}-4}$

Solution: Multiply by the conjugate: $\frac{\sqrt{6}+4}{\sqrt{6}+4} \rightarrow \frac{5}{\sqrt{6}-4} \times \frac{\sqrt{6}+4}{\sqrt{6}+4}$

$(\sqrt{6} - 4)(\sqrt{6} + 4) = -10$, then: $\frac{5}{\sqrt{6}-4} \times \frac{\sqrt{6}+4}{\sqrt{6}+4} = \frac{5(\sqrt{6}+4)}{-10}$

Use the fraction rule: $\frac{a}{-b} = -\frac{a}{b} \rightarrow \frac{5(\sqrt{6}+4)}{-10} = -\frac{5(\sqrt{6}+4)}{10} = -\frac{1}{2}(\sqrt{6} + 4)$

Example 3. Simplify $\frac{2}{\sqrt{3}-1}$

Solution: Multiply by the conjugate: $\frac{\sqrt{3}+1}{\sqrt{3}+1}$

$\frac{2}{\sqrt{3}-1} \times \frac{\sqrt{3}+1}{\sqrt{3}+1} = \frac{2(\sqrt{3}+1)}{2} \rightarrow = (\sqrt{3} + 1)$

Radical Equations

To solve a radical equation:

- Isolate the radical on one side of the equation.

- Square both sides of the equation to remove the radical.

- Solve the equation for the variable.

- Plugin the answer (answers) into the original equation to avoid extraneous values.

Examples:

Example 1. Solve $\sqrt{x} - 5 = 15$

Solution: Add 5 to both sides: $\sqrt{x} = 20$

Square both sides:

$$\left(\sqrt{x}\right)^2 = 20^2 \rightarrow x = 400$$

Plugin the value of 400 for x in the original equation and check the answer:

$$x = 400 \rightarrow \sqrt{x} - 5 = \sqrt{400} - 5 = 20 - 5 = 15$$

So, the value of 400 for x is correct.

Example 2. What is the value of x in this equation?

$$2\sqrt{x + 1} = 4$$

Solution: Divide both sides by 2. Then:

$$2\sqrt{x + 1} = 4 \rightarrow \frac{2\sqrt{x + 1}}{2} = \frac{4}{2} \rightarrow \sqrt{x + 1} = 2$$

Square both sides: $\left(\sqrt{(x + 1)}\right)^2 = 2^2$, Then: $x + 1 = 4 \rightarrow x = 3$

Substitute x by 3 in the original equation and check the answer:

$$x = 3 \rightarrow 2\sqrt{x + 1} = 2\sqrt{3 + 1} = 2\sqrt{4} = 2(2) = 4$$

So, the value of 3 for x is correct.

Domain and Range of Radical Functions

- To find the domain of a radical function, find all possible values of the variable inside radical.

- Remember that having a negative number under the square root symbol is not possible. (For cubic roots, we can have negative numbers)

- To find the range, plugin the minimum and maximum values of the variable inside radical.

Examples:

Example 1. Find the domain and range of the radical function. $y = \sqrt{x - 3}$

Solution: For domain: Find non-negative values for radicals: $x - 3 \geq 0$
Domain of functions: $x - 3 \geq 0 \to x \geq 3$
Domain of the function $y = \sqrt{x - 3}$: $x \geq 3$
For range: The range of a radical function of the form $c\sqrt{ax + b} + k$ is: $f(x) \geq k$
For the function $y = \sqrt{x - 3}$, the value of k is 0. Then: $f(x) \geq 0$
Range of the function $y = \sqrt{x - 3}$: $f(x) \geq 0$

Example 2. Find the domain and range of the radical function. $y = 5\sqrt{3x + 6} + 4$

Solution: For domain: Find non-negative values for radicals: $3x + 6 \geq 0$
Domain of functions: $3x + 6 \geq 0 \to 3x \geq -6 \to x \geq -2$
Domain of the function $y = 5\sqrt{3x + 6} + 4$: $x \geq -2$
For range: The range of a radical function of the form $c\sqrt{ax + b} + k$ is: $f(x) \geq k$
For the function $y = 5\sqrt{3x + 6} + 4$, the value of k is 4. Then: $f(x) \geq 4$
Range of the function $y = 5\sqrt{3x + 6} + 4$: $f(x) \geq 4$

bit.ly/2Pn4vlj
Find more at

Chapter 16: Practices

✍ Simplify.

1) $\sqrt{256y} =$

2) $\sqrt{900} =$

3) $\sqrt{144a^2b} =$

4) $\sqrt{36 \times 9} =$

✍ Simplify.

5) $3\sqrt{5} + 2\sqrt{5} =$

6) $6\sqrt{3} + 4\sqrt{27} =$

7) $5\sqrt{2} + 10\sqrt{18} =$

8) $7\sqrt{2} - 5\sqrt{8} =$

✍ Evaluate.

9) $\sqrt{5} \times \sqrt{3} =$

10) $\sqrt{6} \times \sqrt{8} =$

11) $3\sqrt{5} \times \sqrt{9} =$

12) $2\sqrt{3} \times 3\sqrt{7} =$

✍ Simplify.

13) $\frac{1}{\sqrt{3}-6} =$

14) $\frac{5}{\sqrt{2}+7} =$

15) $\frac{\sqrt{3}}{1-\sqrt{6}} =$

16) $\frac{2}{\sqrt{3}+5} =$

✍ Solve for x.

17) $\sqrt{x} + 2 = 9$

18) $3 + \sqrt{x} = 12$

19) $\sqrt{x} + 5 = 30$

20) $\sqrt{x} - 9 = 27$

21) $10 = \sqrt{x+1}$

22) $\sqrt{x+4} = 3$

✍ Identify the domain and range of each function.

Effortless Math Education

23) $y = \sqrt{x+2} - 1$

24) $y = \sqrt{x+1}$

25) $y = \sqrt{x-4}$

26) $y = \sqrt{x-3} + 1$

Answers – Chapter 16

1) $16\sqrt{y}$

2) 30

3) $12a\sqrt{b}$

4) 18

5) $5\sqrt{5}$

6) $18\sqrt{3}$

7) $35\sqrt{2}$

8) $-3\sqrt{2}$

9) $\sqrt{15}$

10) $\sqrt{48} = 4\sqrt{3}$

11) $9\sqrt{5}$

12) $6\sqrt{21}$

13) $-\frac{\sqrt{3}+6}{33}$

14) $-\frac{5(\sqrt{2}-7)}{47}$

15) $-\frac{\sqrt{3}+3\sqrt{2}}{5}$

16) $-\frac{\sqrt{3}-5}{11}$

17) $x = 49$

18) $x = 81$

19) $x = 625$

20) $x = 1,296$

21) $x = 99$

22) $x = 5$

23) $x \geq -2, y \geq -1$

24) $x \geq -1, y \geq 0$

25) $x \geq 4, y \geq 0$

26) $x \geq 3, y \geq 1$

CHAPTER

17 Circles

Math topics that you'll learn in this chapter:

- ☑ Circumference and Area of Circles
- ☑ Arc length and sector Area
- ☑ Equation of a Circle
- ☑ Finding the Center and the Radius of Circles

159

Circumference and Area of Circles

- In a circle, variable r is usually used for the radius and d for diameter.

- *Area of a circle* $= \pi r^2$ (π is about 3.14)

- *Circumference of a circle* $= 2\pi r$

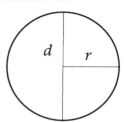

Examples:

Example 1. Find the area of this circle.

Solution:

Use area formula: $Area = \pi r^2$

$r = 8\ in \rightarrow Area = \pi(8)^2 = 64\pi$, $\pi = 3.14$

Then: $Area = 64 \times 3.14 = 200.96\ in^2$

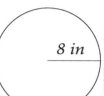

Example 2. Find the Circumference of this circle.

Solution:

Use Circumference formula: $Circumference = 2\pi r$

$r = 5\ cm \rightarrow Circumference = 2\pi(5) = 10\pi$

$\pi = 3.14$ Then: $Circumference = 10 \times 3.14 = 31.4\ cm$

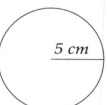

Example 3. Find the area of the circle.

Solution:

Use area formula: $Area = \pi r^2$,

$r = 5\ in$, then: $Area = \pi(5)^2 = 25\pi$, $\pi = 3.14$

Then: $Area = 25 \times 3.14 = 78.5$

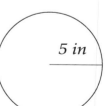

Arc Length and Sector Area

- To find the area of a sector of a circle, use this formula:

    Area of a sector $= \pi r^2 (\frac{\theta}{360})$, r is the radius of the circle and θ is the central angle of the sector.

- To find the arc of a sector of a circle, use this formula:

    Arc of a sector$= (\frac{\theta}{180})\pi r$

Examples:

Example 1. Find the length of the arc. Round your answers to the nearest tenth.
$$(\pi = 3.14), r = 20\ cm, \theta = 30°$$

Solution: Use this formula: Length of the sector $= \left(\frac{\theta}{180}\right)\pi r =$
$\left(\frac{30}{180}\right)\pi(20) = \left(\frac{1}{6}\right)\pi(20) = \left(\frac{20}{6}\right) \times 3.14 \cong 10.5\ cm$

Example 2. Find the area of the sector. $(\pi = 3.14)$ r = 6 ft, $\theta = 70°$

Solution: Use this formula: area of a sector $= \pi r^2(\frac{\theta}{360})$

Area of the sector $= \pi r^2 \left(\frac{\theta}{360}\right) = (3.14)(6^2)\left(\frac{70}{360}\right) = 21.98\ \text{ft}^2$

Example 3. Find the length of the arc. $(\pi = 3.14)$ r = 3 ft, $\theta = \frac{\pi}{3}$

Solution: $\theta = \frac{\pi}{3} \rightarrow \frac{\pi}{3} \times \frac{180}{\pi} = 60°$

Length of the sector$= \left(\frac{60}{180}\right)\pi(3) = \left(\frac{1}{3}\right)\pi(3) = 1 \times 3.14 = 3.14\ cm$

Equation of a Circle

- Equation of circles in standard form: $(x - h)^2 + (y - k)^2 = r^2$

  Center: (h, k), Radius: r

- Equation of circles in general form: $x^2 + y^2 + Ax + By + C = 0$

Examples:

Write the standard form equation of each circle.

Example 1. $x^2 + y^2 - 4x - 6y + 9 = 0$

Solution: The standard form of circle equation is: $(x - h)^2 + (y - k)^2 = r^2$ where the radius of the circle is r, and it's centered at (h, k).

First, move the loose number to the right side: $x^2 + y^2 - 4x - 6y = -9$

Group x-variables and y-variables together: $(x^2 - 4x) + (y^2 - 6y) = -9$

Convert x to square form:

$(x^2 - 4x + 4) + y^2 - 6y = -9 + 4 \rightarrow (x - 2)^2 + (y^2 - 6y) = -9 + 4$

Convert y to square form:

$(x - 2)^2 + (y^2 - 6y + 9) = -9 + 4 + 9 \rightarrow (x - 2)^2 + (y - 3)^2 = 4$

Then, the equation of the circle in standard form is: $(x - 2)^2 + (y - 3)^2 = 2^2$

Example 2. The center of the circle is at $(-2, -10)$, and its radius is 5.

Solution: $(x - h)^2 + (y - k)^2 = r^2$ is the circle equation with a radius r, centered at (h, k). So, $h = -2$, $k = -10$ and $r = 5$

Then, the equation of the circle is: $(x - (-2))^2 + (y - (-10))^2 = (5)^2$

Finding the Center and the Radius of Circles

To find the center and the radius of a circle using the equation of the circle:

- Write the equation of the circle in standard form: $(x - h)^2 + (y - k)^2 = r^2$,

- The center of the circle is at (h, k), and its radius is r.

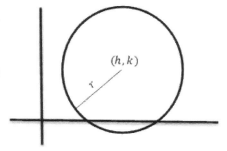

Examples:

Identify the center and the radius of each circle:

Example 1. $x^2 + y^2 - 4x + 3 = 0$

Solution: $(x - h)^2 + (y - k)^2 = r^2$ is the circle equation with a radius r, centered at (h, k).

Rewrite $x^2 + y^2 - 4x + 3 = 0$ in the standard form:

$x^2 + y^2 - 4x + 3 = 0 \rightarrow (x - 2)^2 + y^2 = 1^2$

Then, the center is at: $(2, 0)$ and $r = 1$

Example 2. $8x + x^2 + 10y = 8 - y^2$

Solution: Rewrite the equation in standard form:

$8x + x^2 + 10y = 8 - y^2 \rightarrow (x - (-4))^2 + (y - (-5))^2 = 7^2$

Then, the center is at $(-4, -5)$ and the radius is 7.

Chapter 17: Practices

🖎 Complete the table below. ($\pi = 3.14$)

1)	Radius	Diameter	Circumference	Area
Circle 1	3 inches	6 inches	18.84 inches	28.26 square inches
Circle 2			43.96 meters	
Circle 3		8 ft		
Circle 4				78.5 square miles

🖎 Find the length of each arc. Round your answers to the nearest hundredth.

2) $r = 4 \text{ cm}, \theta = 28° \rightarrow$ arc =

3) $r = 6 \text{ ft}, \theta = 30° \rightarrow$ arc =

4) $r = 8 \text{ ft}, \theta = 40° \rightarrow$ arc =

5) $r = 12 \text{ cm}, \theta = 34° \rightarrow$ arc =

🖎 Write the standard form equation of each circle.

6) $x^2 + y^2 - 4x + 2y - 4 = 0 \rightarrow$

7) $x^2 + y^2 - 8x + 6y - 11 = 0 \rightarrow$

8) $x^2 + y^2 - 10x - 12y + 12 = 0 \rightarrow$

9) $x^2 + y^2 + 12x - 6y - 19 = 0 \rightarrow$

10) $x^2 + y^2 - 6x + 8y + 24 = 0 \rightarrow$

🖎 Identify the center and radius of each circle.

11) $(x + 1)^2 + (y - 2)^2 = 5 \rightarrow$ Center: (___,___) Radius: _____

12) $(x - 5)^2 + (y + 10)^2 = 4 \rightarrow$ Center: (___,___) Radius: _____

13) $x^2 + (y - 3)^2 = 8 \rightarrow$ Center: (___,___) Radius: _____

14) $(x - 1)^2 + y^2 = 9 \rightarrow$ Center: (___,___) Radius: _____

15) $x^2 + y^2 = 16 \rightarrow$ Center: (___,___) Radius: _____

16) $(x + 1)^2 + (y + 6)^2 = 10 \rightarrow$ Center: (___,___) Radius: _____

Answers – Chapter 17

1)	Radius	Diameter	Circumference	Area
Circle 1	3 inches	6 inches	18.84 inches	28.26 square inches
Circle 2	7 meters	14 meters	43.96 meters	153.86 square meters
Circle 3	4 ft	8 ft	25.12 ft	50.24 square ft
Circle 4	5 miles	10 miles	31.4 miles	78.5 square miles

2) $1.95\ cm$

3) $3.14\ ft$

4) $5.58\ ft$

5) $7.12\ cm$

6) $(x-2)^2 + (y-(-1))^2 = 3^2$

7) $(x-4)^2 + (y-(-3))^2 = 6^2$

8) $(x-5)^2 + (y-6)^2 = 7^2$

9) $(x-(-6))^2 + (y-3)^2 = 8^2$

10) $(x-3)^2 + (y-(-4))^2 = 1^2$

11) Center: $(-1, 2)$, Radius: $\sqrt{5}$

12) Center: $(5, -10)$, Radius: 2

13) Center: $(0, 3)$, Radius: $2\sqrt{2}$

14) Center: $(1, 0)$, Radius: 3

15) Center: $(0, 0)$, Radius: 4

16) Center: $(-1, -6)$, Radius: $\sqrt{10}$

**Effortless
Math
Education**

18 Rational Expressions

Math topics that you'll learn in this chapter:

- ☑ Simplifying Complex Fractions
- ☑ Graphing Rational Expressions
- ☑ Adding and Subtracting Rational Expressions
- ☑ Multiplying Rational Expressions
- ☑ Dividing Rational Expressions
- ☑ Rational Equations

167

Simplifying Complex Fractions

- Convert mixed numbers to improper fractions.

- Simplify all fractions.

- Write the fraction in the numerator of the main fraction line then write division sign (÷) and the fraction of the denominator.

- Use normal method for dividing fractions.

- Simplify as needed.

Examples:

Example 1. Simplify: $\dfrac{\frac{3}{5}}{\frac{2}{25}-\frac{5}{16}}$

Solution: First, simplify the denominator: $\dfrac{2}{25}-\dfrac{5}{16}=-\dfrac{93}{400}$,

Then: $\dfrac{\frac{3}{5}}{\frac{2}{25}-\frac{5}{16}}=\dfrac{\frac{3}{5}}{-\frac{93}{400}}$; Now, write the complex fraction using the division sign:

$\dfrac{\frac{3}{5}}{\frac{93}{400}}=\dfrac{3}{5}\div\left(-\dfrac{93}{400}\right)$. Use the dividing fractions rule: Keep, Change, Flip (keep the

first fraction, change the division sign to multiplication, flip the second fraction)

$$\frac{3}{5}\div\left(-\frac{93}{400}\right)=\frac{3}{5}\times\frac{400}{93}=-\frac{240}{93}=-\frac{80}{31}=2\frac{18}{31}$$

Example 2. Simplify: $\dfrac{\frac{2}{5}\div\frac{1}{3}}{\frac{5}{9}+\frac{1}{3}}$

Solution: First, simplify the numerator: $\dfrac{2}{5}\div\dfrac{1}{3}=\dfrac{6}{5}$, then, simplify the

denominator: $\dfrac{5}{9}+\dfrac{1}{3}=\dfrac{8}{9}$, Now, write the complex fraction using the division

sign (÷): $\dfrac{\frac{2}{5}\div\frac{1}{3}}{\frac{5}{9}+\frac{1}{3}}=\dfrac{\frac{6}{5}}{\frac{8}{9}}=\dfrac{6}{5}\div\dfrac{8}{9}$, Use the dividing fractions rule: (Keep,

Change, Flip) $\dfrac{6}{5}\div\dfrac{8}{9}=\dfrac{6}{5}\times\dfrac{9}{8}=\dfrac{54}{40}=\dfrac{27}{20}=1\dfrac{7}{20}$

Graphing Rational Expressions

- A rational expression is a fraction in which the numerator and/or the denominator are polynomials. Examples: $\frac{1}{x}, \frac{x^2}{x-1}, \frac{x^2-x+2}{x^2+5x+1}, \frac{m^2+6m-5}{m-2m}$
- To graph a rational function:

   o Find the vertical asymptotes of the function if there is any. (Vertical asymptotes are vertical lines which correspond to the zeroes of the denominator. The graph will have a vertical asymptote at $x = a$ if the denominator is zero at $x = a$ and the numerator isn't zero at $x = a$)

   o Find the horizontal or slant asymptote. (If the numerator has a bigger degree than the denominator, there will be a slant asymptote. To find the slant asymptote, divide the numerator by the denominator using either long division or synthetic division.)

   o If the denominator has a bigger degree than the numerator, the horizontal asymptote is the x-axes or the line $y = 0$. If they have the same degree, the horizontal asymptote equals the leading coefficient (the coefficient of the largest exponent) of the numerator divided by the leading coefficient of the denominator.

   o Find intercepts and plug in some values of x and solve for y, then graph the function.

Example:

Graph rational function. $f(x) = \frac{x^2-x+2}{x-1}$

Solution: First, notice that the graph is in two pieces. Most rational functions have graphs in multiple pieces. Find $y - intercept$ by substituting zero for x and solving for y ($f(x)$): $x = 0 \rightarrow y = \frac{x^2-x+2}{x-1} = \frac{0^2-0+2}{0-1} = -2$,

$$y - intercept: (0, -2)$$

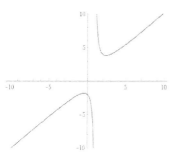

Asymptotes of $\frac{x^2-x+2}{x-1}$: Vertical: $x = 1$, Slant asymptote: $y = 2x + 1$ (divide the numerator by the denominator). After finding the asymptotes, you can plug in some values for x and solve for y. Here is the sketch for this function.

bit.ly/2PmZoI8

Find more at

Adding and Subtracting Rational Expressions

For adding and subtracting rational expressions:

- Find least common denominator (LCD).

- Write each expression using the LCD.

- Add or subtract the numerators.

- Simplify as needed.

Examples:

Example 1. Solve. $\frac{4}{2x+3} + \frac{x-2}{2x+3} =$

Solution: The denominators are equal. Then, use fractions addition rule:

$$\frac{a}{c} \pm \frac{b}{c} = \frac{a \pm b}{c} \rightarrow \frac{4}{2x+3} + \frac{x-2}{2x+3} = \frac{4+(x-2)}{2x+3} = \frac{x+2}{2x+3}$$

Example 2. Solve. $\frac{x+4}{x-5} + \frac{x-4}{x+6} =$

Solution: Find the least common denominator of $(x-5)$ and $(x+6)$: $(x-5)(x+6)$

Then: $\frac{x+4}{x-5} + \frac{x-4}{x+6} = \frac{(x+4)(x+6)}{(x-5)(x+6)} + \frac{(x-4)(x-5)}{(x+6)(x-5)} = \frac{(x+4)(x+6)+(x-4)(x-5)}{(x+6)(x-5)}$

Expand: $(x+4)(x+6) + (x-4)(x-5) = 2x^2 + x + 44$

Then: $\frac{(x+4)(x+6)+(x-4)(x-5)}{(x+6)(x-5)} = \frac{2x^2+x+44}{(x+6)(x-5)} = \frac{2x^2+x+44}{x^2+x-30}$

Multiplying Rational Expressions

- Multiplying rational expressions is the same as multiplying fractions. First, multiply numerators and then multiply denominators. Then, simplify as needed.

Examples:

Example 1. Solve: $\frac{x+6}{x-1} \times \frac{x-1}{5} =$

Solution: Multiply numerators and denominators: $\frac{a}{b} \times \frac{c}{d} = \frac{a \times c}{b \times d}$

$$\frac{x+6}{x-1} \times \frac{x-1}{5} = \frac{(x+6)(x-1)}{5(x-1)}$$

Cancel the common factor: $(x-1)$

Then: $\frac{(x+6)(x-1)}{5(x-1)} = \frac{(x+6)}{5}$

Example 2. Solve: $\frac{x-2}{x+3} \times \frac{2x+6}{x-2} =$

Solution: Multiply numerators and denominators: $\frac{x-2}{x+3} \times \frac{2x+6}{x-2} = \frac{(x-2)(2x+6)}{(x+3)(x-2)}$

Cancel the common factor: $\frac{(x-2)(2x+6)}{(x+3)(x-2)} = \frac{(2x+6)}{(x+3)}$

Factor $2x + 6 = 2(x+3)$

Then: $\frac{2(x+3)}{(x+3)} = 2$

bit.ly/3fcliIU

Find more at

Dividing Rational Expressions

- To divide rational expressions, use the same method we use for dividing fractions. (Keep, Change, Flip)

- Keep the first rational expression, change the division sign to multiplication, and flip the numerator and denominator of the second rational expression. Then, multiply numerators and multiply denominators. Simplify as needed.

Examples:

Example 1. Solve. $\frac{x+2}{3x} \div \frac{x^2+5x+6}{3x^2+3x} =$

Solution: Use fractions division rule: $\frac{a}{b} \div \frac{c}{d} = \frac{a}{b} \times \frac{d}{c} = \frac{a \times d}{b \times c}$

$$\frac{x+2}{3x} \div \frac{x^2+5x+6}{3x^2+3x} = \frac{x+2}{3x} \times \frac{3x^2+3x}{x^2+5x+6} = \frac{(x+2)(3x^2+3x)}{(3x)(x^2+5x+6)}$$

Now, factorize the expressions $3x^2 + 3x$ and $(x^2 + 5x + 6)$. Then:

$3x^2 + 3x = 3x(x + 1)$ and $x^2 + 5x + 6 = (x + 2)(x + 3)$

Simplify: $\frac{(x+2)(3x^2+3x)}{(3x)(x^2+5x+6)} = \frac{(x+2)(3x)(x+1)}{(3x)(x+2)(x+3)}$, cancel common factors. Then:

$$\frac{(x+2)(3x)(x+1)}{(3x)(x+2)(x+3)} = \frac{x+1}{x+3}$$

Example 2. Solve. $\frac{5x}{x+3} \div \frac{x}{2x+6} =$

Solution: Use fractions division rule: $\frac{a}{b} \div \frac{c}{d} = \frac{a}{b} \times \frac{d}{c} = \frac{a \times d}{b \times c}$

Then: $\frac{5x}{x+3} \div \frac{x}{2x+6} = \frac{5x}{x+3} \times \frac{2x+6}{x} = \frac{5x(2x+6)}{x(x+3)} = \frac{5x \times 2(x+3)}{x(x+3)}$

Cancel common factor: $\frac{5x \times 2(x+3)}{x(x+3)} = \frac{10x(x+3)}{x(x+3)} = 10$

Rational Equations

For solving rational equations, we can use following methods:

- **Converting to a common denominator:** In this method, you need to get a common denominator for both sides of the equation. Then, make numerators equal and solve for the variable.

- **Cross-multiplying:** This method is useful when there is only one fraction on each side of the equation. Simply multiply the first numerator by the second denominator and make the result equal to the product of the second numerator and the first denominator.

Examples:

Example 1. Solve. $\frac{x-2}{x+1} = \frac{x+4}{x-2}$

Solution: Use cross multiply method: if $\frac{a}{b} = \frac{c}{d}$, then: $a \times d = b \times c$

$\frac{x-2}{x+1} = \frac{x+4}{x-2} \rightarrow (x-2)(x-2) = (x+4)(x+1)$

Expand: $(x-2)^2 = x^2 - 4x + 4$ and $(x+4)(x+1) = x^2 + 5x + 4$,

Then: $x^2 - 4x + 4 = x^2 + 5x + 4$, Now, simplify: $x^2 - 4x = x^2 + 5x$, subtract both sides $(x^2 + 5x)$,

Then: $x^2 - 4x - (x^2 + 5x) = x^2 + 5x - (x^2 + 5x) \rightarrow -9x = 0 \rightarrow x = 0$

Example 2. Solve. $\frac{2x}{x-3} = \frac{2x+2}{2x-6}$

Solution: Multiply the numerator and denominator of the rational expression on the left by 2 to get a common denominator $(2x - 6)$. $\frac{2(2x)}{2(x-3)} = \frac{4x}{2x-6}$

Now, the denominators on both side of the equation are equal. Therefore, their numerators must be equal too.

$$\frac{4x}{2x-6} = \frac{2x+2}{2x-6} \rightarrow 4x = 2x+2 \rightarrow 2x = 2 \rightarrow x = 1$$

Chapter 18: Practices

✍ Simplify each expression.

1) $\dfrac{\frac{2}{5}}{\frac{4}{7}} =$

2) $\dfrac{6}{\frac{5}{x}+\frac{2}{3x}} =$

3) $\dfrac{1-\frac{2}{x-1}}{1+\frac{4}{x+1}} =$

4) $\dfrac{x}{\frac{3}{4}-\frac{5}{x}} =$

✍ Graph rational expressions.

5) $f(x) = \dfrac{x^2}{5x+6}$

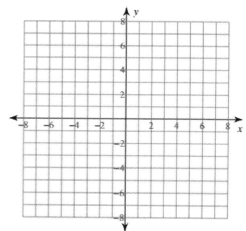

6) $f(x) = \dfrac{x^2+8x+10}{x+5}$

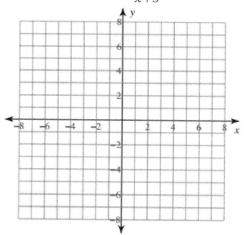

✍ Simplify each expression.

7) $\dfrac{5}{x+2} + \dfrac{x-1}{x+2} =$

8) $\dfrac{6}{x+5} - \dfrac{5}{x+5} =$

9) $\dfrac{7}{4x+10} + \dfrac{x-5}{4x+10} =$

✍ Simplify each expression.

10) $\dfrac{x+1}{x+5} \times \dfrac{x+6}{x+1} =$

11) $\dfrac{x+4}{x+9} \times \dfrac{x+9}{x+3} =$

12) $\dfrac{x+8}{x} \times \dfrac{2}{x+8} =$

13) $\dfrac{x+5}{x+1} \times \dfrac{x^2}{x+5} =$

14) $\dfrac{x-3}{x+2} \times \dfrac{2x+4}{x+4} =$

15) $\dfrac{x-6}{x+3} \times \dfrac{2x+6}{2x} =$

✍ Solve.

16) $\dfrac{5x}{4} \div \dfrac{5}{2} =$

17) $\dfrac{8}{3x} \div \dfrac{24}{x} =$

18) $\dfrac{3x}{x+4} \div \dfrac{x}{3x+12} =$

19) $\dfrac{2}{5x} \div \dfrac{16}{10x} =$

20) $\dfrac{36x}{5} \div \dfrac{4}{3} =$

21) $\dfrac{15x^2}{6} \div \dfrac{5x}{14} =$

✍ Solve each equation.

22) $\dfrac{1}{8x^2} = \dfrac{1}{4x^2} - \dfrac{1}{x} \rightarrow x = $ _____

23) $\dfrac{1}{x} + \dfrac{1}{9x} = \dfrac{5}{36} \rightarrow x = $ _____

24) $\dfrac{32}{2x^2} + 1 = \dfrac{8}{x} \rightarrow x = $ _____

25) $\dfrac{1}{x-5} = \dfrac{4}{x-5} + 1 \rightarrow x = $ _____

Effortless
Math
Education

Answers – Chapter 18

1) $\frac{7}{10}$

2) $\frac{18x}{17}$

3) $\frac{x^2-2x-3}{x^2+4x-5}$

4) $\frac{4x^2}{3x-20}$

5)

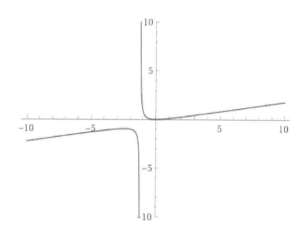

6)

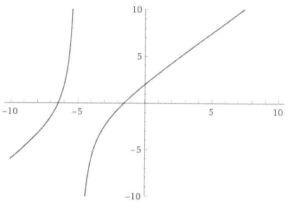

7) $\frac{x+4}{x+2}$

8) $\frac{1}{x+5}$

9) $\frac{x+2}{4x+10}$

10) $\frac{x+6}{x+5}$

11) $\frac{x+4}{x+3}$

12) $\frac{2}{x}$

13) $\frac{x^2}{x+1}$

14) $\frac{2(x-3)}{x+4}$

15) $\frac{x-6}{x}$

16) $\frac{x}{2}$

17) $\frac{1}{9}$

18) 9

19) $\frac{1}{4}$

20) $\frac{27x}{5}$

21) $7x$

22) $x = \frac{1}{8}$

23) $x = 8$

24) $x = 4$

25) $x = 2$

Effortless Math Education

CHAPTER

19 Trigonometric Functions

Math topics that you'll learn in this Chapter:

- ☑ Angle and Angle Measure
- ☑ Trigonometric Functions
- ☑ Coterminal Angles and Reference Angles
- ☑ Evaluating Trigonometric Functions
- ☑ Missing Sides and Angles of a Right Triangle

177

Angle and Angle Measure

- To convert degrees to radians, use this formula:

Radians = Degrees × $\frac{\pi}{180}$

- To convert radians to degrees, use this formula:

Degrees = Radians × $\frac{180}{\pi}$

Examples:

Example 1. Convert 160 degrees to radian.

Solution: Use this formula: Radians = Degrees × $\frac{\pi}{180}$

Radians = $160 \times \frac{\pi}{180} = \frac{160\pi}{180} = \frac{8\pi}{9}$

Example 2. Convert radian measure $\frac{3\pi}{4}$ to degree measure.

Solution: Use this formula: Degrees = Radians × $\frac{180}{\pi}$

Radians = $\frac{3\pi}{4} \times \frac{180}{\pi} = \frac{540\pi}{4\pi} = 135$

Example 3. Convert 150 degrees to radian.

Solution: Use this formula: Radians = Degrees × $\frac{\pi}{180}$

Radians = $150 \times \frac{\pi}{180} = \frac{150\pi}{180} = \frac{5\pi}{6}$

Example 4. Convert radian measure $\frac{2\pi}{3}$ to degree measure.

Solution: Use this formula: Degrees = Radians × $\frac{180}{\pi}$

Radians = $\frac{2\pi}{3} \times \frac{180}{\pi} = \frac{360\pi}{3\pi} = 120$

bit.ly/3pxMlAh

Find more at

Trigonometric Functions

- Trigonometric functions refer to the relation between the sides and angles of a right triangle. There are 6 trigonometric functions:

- Sine (sin), Cosine (cos), Tangent (tan), Secant (sec), Cosecant (csc), and Cotangent (cot)

- The three main trigonometric functions:

$$SOH - CAH - TOA, \ sin \ \theta = \frac{opposite}{hypotenuse}, \ Cos \ \theta = \frac{adjacent}{hypotenuse}, \ tan \ \theta = \frac{opposite}{adjacent}$$

- The reciprocal trigonometric functions:

$$csc \ x = \frac{1}{sin \ x}, \ sec \ x = \frac{1}{cos \ x}, \ cot \ \theta = \frac{1}{tan \ x}$$

- Learn common trigonometric functions:

θ	0°	30°	45°	60°	90°
$sin \ \theta$	0	$\frac{1}{2}$	$\frac{\sqrt{2}}{2}$	$\frac{\sqrt{3}}{2}$	1
$cos \ \theta$	1	$\frac{\sqrt{3}}{2}$	$\frac{\sqrt{2}}{2}$	$\frac{1}{2}$	0
$tan \ \theta$	0	$\frac{\sqrt{3}}{3}$	1	$\sqrt{3}$	Undefined

Examples:

Find each trigonometric function.

Example 1. $sin \ 120°$

Solution: Use the following property: $sin(x) = cos(90° - x)$

$sin \ 120° = cos(90° - 120°) = cos(-30°) = \frac{\sqrt{3}}{2}$

Example 2. $tan \ 120°$

Solution: Use the following property: $tan(x) = \frac{sin \ (x)}{cos \ (x)}$

$tan(x) = \frac{sin(x)}{cos(x)} = tan(120) = \frac{sin(120)}{cos(120)} = \frac{\frac{\sqrt{3}}{2}}{-\frac{1}{2}} = -\sqrt{3}$

Coterminal Angles and Reference Angles

- Coterminal angles are equal angles.

- To find a Coterminal of an angle, add or subtract 360 degrees (or 2π for radians) to the given angle.

- Reference angle is the smallest angle that you can make from the terminal side of an angle with the x-axis.

Examples:

Example 1. Find a positive and a negative Coterminal angle to angle $65°$.

Solution:

$65° - 360° = -295°$

$65° + 360° = 425°$

$-295°$ and a $425°$ are Coterminal with angle $65°$.

Example 2. Find positive and negative Coterminal angles to angle $\frac{\pi}{2}$.

Solution:

$\frac{\pi}{2} + 2\pi = \frac{5\pi}{2}$

$\frac{\pi}{2} - 2\pi = -\frac{3\pi}{2}$

Example 3. Find a positive and a negative Coterminal angle to angle $80°$.

Solution:

$80° - 360° = -280°$

$80° + 360° = 440°$

$-280°$ and a $440°$ are Coterminal with angle $80°$.

Evaluating Trigonometric Functions

- **Step 1:** Find the reference angle. (It is the smallest angle that you can make from the terminal side of an angle with the x-axis.)

- **Step 2:** Determine the quadrant of the function. Depending on the quadrant in which the function lies, the answer will be either positive or negative.

- **Step 3:** Find the trigonometric function of the reference angle.

Examples:

Example 1. Find the exact value of trigonometric function. $tan\ \frac{5\pi}{4}$

Solution: Rewrite the angle for $\frac{5\pi}{4}$:

$tan\ \frac{5\pi}{4} = tan\left(\frac{4\pi+\pi}{4}\right) = tan\left(\pi + \frac{1}{4}\pi\right)$

Use the periodicity of tan: $tan(x + \pi . k) = tan(x)$

$tan\left(\pi + \frac{1}{4}\pi\right) = tan\left(\frac{1}{4}\pi\right) = 1$

Example 2. Find the exact value of trigonometric function. $cos\ 225°$

Solution: First, recall that $cos(225°)$ is in the third quadrant and cosine is negative in the third quadrant.

The reference angle of $225°$ is $45°$. Therefore, $cos\ 225° = -cos\ 45°$

$cos\ 45° = \frac{\sqrt{2}}{2}$. Then, $-cos\ 45° = -\frac{\sqrt{2}}{2}$

Example 3. Find the exact value of trigonometric function. $sin\ \frac{7\pi}{6}$

Solution: Rewrite the $sin\ \frac{7\pi}{6}$.

$sin\ \frac{7\pi}{6} = sin\left(\frac{\pi}{6} + \pi\right) = cos\left(\frac{\pi}{6}\right)$ (complementary arcs)

Trig Table of Special Arcs gives: $cos\ \frac{\pi}{6} = \frac{\sqrt{3}}{2}$

bit.ly/3aUyyQy
Find more at

Missing Sides and Angles of a Right Triangle

- By using three main trigonometric functions (Sine, Cosine or Tangent), we can find an unknown side in a right triangle when we have one length, and one angle (apart from the right angle).

- A right triangle with Adjacent and Opposite sides and Hypotenuse is shown below.

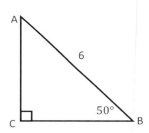

- Recall the three main trigonometric functions:

  SOH – CAH – TOA, $sin\,\theta = \frac{opposite}{hypotenuse}$, $Cos\,\theta = \frac{adjacent}{hypotenuse}$, $tan\,\theta = \frac{opposite}{adjacent}$

- To find missing angles, use inverse of trigonometric functions (examples: $sin^{-1}, cos^{-1}, and\ tan^{-1}$)

Examples:

Example 1. Find side AC in the following triangle. Round your answer to the nearest tenth.

Solution: $sin\,\theta = \frac{opposite}{hypotenuse}$. $sine\,50° = \frac{AC}{6} \rightarrow 6 \times sin\,50° = AC$,

Now use a calculator to find $sin\,50°$.

$$sine\,50° \approx 0.766$$

$AC = 6 \times 0.766 = 4.596$, rounding to the nearest tenth: $4.596 \approx 4.6$

Example 2. Find the value of x in the following triangle.

Solution: $cos\,\theta = \frac{adjacent}{hypotenuse} \rightarrow cos\,x = \frac{10}{14} = \frac{5}{7}$

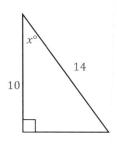

Use a calculator to find inverse cosine:

$$cos^{-1}\left(\frac{5}{7}\right) = 44.41° \approx 44°$$

Then: $x = 44$

Chapter 19: Practices

 **Convert each degree measure into radians.**

1) $135° =$

2) $80° =$

3) $270° =$

4) $92° =$

 **Evaluate.**

5) $sin\ 90° =$ _____

6) $sin -330° =$ _____

7) $tan -30° =$ _____

8) $cot\frac{2\pi}{3} =$ _____

9) $tan\frac{\pi}{3} =$ _____

10) $sin\frac{2\pi}{6} =$ _____

 **Find a positive and a negative Coterminal angle for each angle.**

11) $140° =$

   Positive = _____

   Negative = _____

12) $-165° =$

   Positive = _____

   Negative = _____

13) $190° =$

   Positive = _____

   Negative = _____

14) $\frac{5\pi}{4} =$

   Positive = _____

   Negative = _____

15) $\frac{2\pi}{9} =$

   Positive = _____

   Negative = _____

16) $-\frac{7\pi}{9} =$

   Positive = _____

   Negative = _____

Effortless
Math
Education

✎ Find the exact value of each trigonometric function.

17) $\cos 180° =$ _____

18) $\cos -270° =$ _____

19) $\tan 225° =$ _____

20) $\quad \sin \frac{\pi}{4} =$ _____

21) $\csc 330° =$ _____

22) $\tan -120° =$ _____

✎ Find the value of x in each triangle.

23) _____

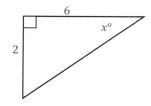

24) _____

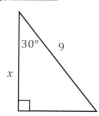

25) _____

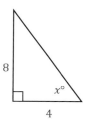

26) _____

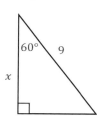

27) _____

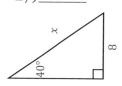

28) _____

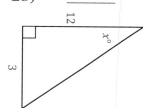

Effortless

Math

Education

Answers – Chapter 19

1) $\frac{3}{4}\pi$

2) $\frac{4}{9}\pi$

3) $\frac{3}{2}\pi$

4) $\frac{23}{45}\pi$

5) 1

6) $\frac{1}{2}$

7) $-\frac{\sqrt{3}}{3}$

8) $-\frac{\sqrt{3}}{3}$

9) $\sqrt{3}$

10) $\frac{\sqrt{3}}{2}$

11) Positive = $500°$, Negative = $-220°$

12) Positive = $195°$, Negative = $-525°$

13) Positive = $550°$, Negative = $-170°$

14) Positive = $\frac{13\pi}{4}$, Negative = $-\frac{3\pi}{4}$

15) Positive = $\frac{20\pi}{9}$, Negative = $-\frac{16\pi}{9}$

16) Positive = $\frac{11\pi}{9}$, Negative = $-\frac{25\pi}{9}$

17) -1

18) 0

19) 1

20) $\frac{\sqrt{2}}{2}$

21) -2

22) $\sqrt{3}$

23) 18

24) 7.8

25) 63

26) 4.5

27) 12.45

28) 14

Time to Test

Time to refine your skill with a practice examination

In this section, there are two complete PSAT Mathematics practice tests. Take these tests to simulate the test day experience. After you've finished, score your tests using the answer keys.

Before You Start

- You'll need a pencil, a timer and a calculator to take the tests.

- There are two types of questions:

  Multiple choice questions: for each of these questions, there are four or more possible answers. Choose which one is best.

  Grid-ins questions: for these questions, you have to fill your answer into a grid.

- It's okay to guess. You won't lose any points if you're wrong.

- The PSAT Mathematics test contains a formula sheet, which displays formulas relating to geometric measurement and certain algebra concepts. Formulas are provided to test-takers so that they may focus on application, rather than the memorization, of formulas.

- After you've finished the test, review the answer key to see where you went wrong and what areas you need to improve.

Good Luck!

PSAT Math Practice Test 1

2022 - 2023

Two Parts

Total number of questions: 48

Section 1 (No Calculator): 17 questions

Section 2 (Calculator): 31 questions

Total time for two parts: 70 Minutes

PSAT Practice Test 1 Answer Sheet

Remove (or photocopy) the answer sheets and use it to complete the practice tests.

PSAT Practice Test 1 – Section 1 Answer Sheet

1 Ⓐ Ⓑ Ⓒ Ⓓ   4 Ⓐ Ⓑ Ⓒ Ⓓ   7 Ⓐ Ⓑ Ⓒ Ⓓ   10 Ⓐ Ⓑ Ⓒ Ⓓ   13 Ⓐ Ⓑ Ⓒ Ⓓ

2 Ⓐ Ⓑ Ⓒ Ⓓ   5 Ⓐ Ⓑ Ⓒ Ⓓ   8 Ⓐ Ⓑ Ⓒ Ⓓ   11 Ⓐ Ⓑ Ⓒ Ⓓ

3 Ⓐ Ⓑ Ⓒ Ⓓ   6 Ⓐ Ⓑ Ⓒ Ⓓ   9 Ⓐ Ⓑ Ⓒ Ⓓ   12 Ⓐ Ⓑ Ⓒ Ⓓ

14   15   16   17

PSAT Practice Test 1 – Section 2 Answer Sheet

1 Ⓐ Ⓑ Ⓒ Ⓓ	7 Ⓐ Ⓑ Ⓒ Ⓓ	13 Ⓐ Ⓑ Ⓒ Ⓓ	19 Ⓐ Ⓑ Ⓒ Ⓓ	25 Ⓐ Ⓑ Ⓒ Ⓓ
2 Ⓐ Ⓑ Ⓒ Ⓓ	8 Ⓐ Ⓑ Ⓒ Ⓓ	14 Ⓐ Ⓑ Ⓒ Ⓓ	20 Ⓐ Ⓑ Ⓒ Ⓓ	26 Ⓐ Ⓑ Ⓒ Ⓓ
3 Ⓐ Ⓑ Ⓒ Ⓓ	9 Ⓐ Ⓑ Ⓒ Ⓓ	15 Ⓐ Ⓑ Ⓒ Ⓓ	21 Ⓐ Ⓑ Ⓒ Ⓓ	27 Ⓐ Ⓑ Ⓒ Ⓓ
4 Ⓐ Ⓑ Ⓒ Ⓓ	10 Ⓐ Ⓑ Ⓒ Ⓓ	16 Ⓐ Ⓑ Ⓒ Ⓓ	22 Ⓐ Ⓑ Ⓒ Ⓓ	
5 Ⓐ Ⓑ Ⓒ Ⓓ	11 Ⓐ Ⓑ Ⓒ Ⓓ	17 Ⓐ Ⓑ Ⓒ Ⓓ	23 Ⓐ Ⓑ Ⓒ Ⓓ	
6 Ⓐ Ⓑ Ⓒ Ⓓ	12 Ⓐ Ⓑ Ⓒ Ⓓ	18 Ⓐ Ⓑ Ⓒ Ⓓ	24 Ⓐ Ⓑ Ⓒ Ⓓ	

28   29   30   31

PSAT Math Practice Test 1

Section 1

(No Calculator)

17 questions

Total time for this section: 25 Minutes

You May NOT use a calculator on this Section.

Reference Sheet

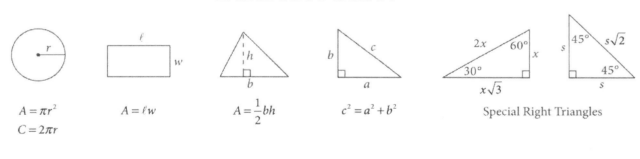

$A = \pi r^2$

$C = 2\pi r$

$A = \ell w$

$A = \dfrac{1}{2}bh$

$c^2 = a^2 + b^2$

Special Right Triangles

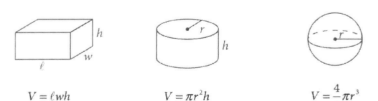

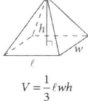

$V = \ell wh$

$V = \pi r^2 h$

$V = \dfrac{4}{3}\pi r^3$

$V = \dfrac{1}{3}\pi r^2 h$

$V = \dfrac{1}{3}\ell wh$

The number of degrees of arc in a circle is 360.

The number of radians of arc in a circle is 2π.

The sum of the measures in degrees of the angles of a triangle is 180.

1) If $5x - 8 = 4.5$, what is the value of $3x + 3$?

A. 10.5

B. 12.5

C. 15.5

D. 25

2) If the function f is defined by $f(x) = x^2 + 2x - 10$, which of the following is equivalent to $f(4t^2)$?

A. $3t^4 + 6t^2 - 10$

B. $16t^4 + 8t^2 - 10$

C. $3t^4 + 3t^2 - 10$

D. $3t^4 + 6t^2 + 10$

3) If $xp + 2yq = 27$ and $xp + yq = 18$, what is the value of yq?

A. 6

B. 7

C. 8

D. 9

4) The circle graph below shows all Nicole's expenses for last month. If she spent $770 on her car, how much did Nicole spend for her rent?

A. $700

B. $740

C. $880

D. $945

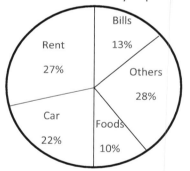

Nicole's monthly expenses

5) If $a^2 + 6$ and $a^2 - 6$ are two factors of the polynomial $30a^4 + b$ and b is a constant, what is the value of b?

A. 36

B. 24

C. -360

D. -1080

$$0.\,ABC \qquad\qquad 0.0D$$

6) The letters represent two decimals listed above. One of the decimals is equivalent to $\frac{3}{8}$ and the other is equivalent to $\frac{2}{25}$. What is the product of C and D?

A. 0

B. 5

C. 40

D. 60

7) In the diagram below, circle A represents the set of all even numbers, circle B represents the set of all negative numbers, and circle C represents the set of all multiples of 6. Which number could be replaced with y?

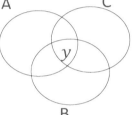

A. 6

B. 0

C. -6

D. -10

8) There are only red and blue cards in a box. The probability of choosing a red card in the box at random is one third. If there are 246 blue cards, how many cards are in the box?

A. 123

B. 308

C. 328

D. 369

9) Both $(x = -2)$ and $(x = 5)$ are solutions for which of the following equations?

$$\text{I. } x^2 - 3x - 25 = 0$$

$$\text{II. } 2x^2 - 6x = 20$$

$$\text{III. } 4x^2 - 12x - 40 = 0$$

A. II only

B. I and II

C. II and III

D. I, II and III

10) The radius of circle A is three times the radius of circle B. If the circumference of circle A is 24π, what is the area of circle B?

A. 3π

B. 6π

C. 16π

D. 18π

11) In a certain bookshelf of a library, there are 30 biology books, 90 history books, and 60 language books. What is the ratio of the number of biology books to the total number of books in this bookshelf?

A. $\frac{1}{4}$

B. $\frac{1}{6}$

C. $\frac{2}{7}$

D. $\frac{3}{8}$

12) In the figure below, what is the value of x?

A. 43

B. 83

C. 87

D. 90

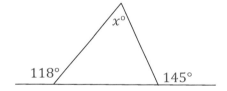

13) The following table represents the value of x and function $f(x)$. Which of the following could be the equation of the function $f(x)$?

A. $f(x) = x^2 - 5$

B. $f(x) = x^2 - 1$

C. $f(x) = \sqrt{x + 2}$

D. $f(x) = \sqrt{x} + 3$

x	$f(x)$
1	4
4	5
9	6
16	7

Grid-ins Questions

Questions 14–17 are grid-ins questions. Solve the problems and enter your answers in the grid on the answer sheet as shown below.

Answer: 3.72

Answer: $\frac{6}{7}$

Write answers in the boxes

Grid in results

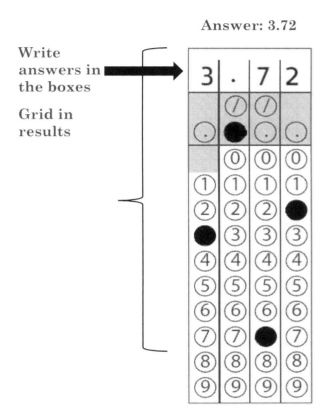

14) Mia and Moe can finish a job together in 120 minutes. If Mia can do the job by herself in 5 hours, how many minutes does it take Moe to finish the job?

15) In the following figure, point O is the center of the circle and the equilateral triangle has perimeter 45. What is the circumference of the circle? ($\pi = 3$)

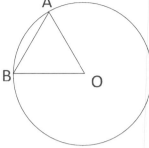

16) If 14% of x is 84 and $\frac{1}{8}$ of y is 18, what is the value of $x - y$?

17) Angle a is 630 degrees and can be written $x\pi$ in radian. What is the value of x?

STOP

This is the End of this Section. You may check your work on this section if you still have time.

PSAT Math Practice Test 1

Section 2

(Calculator)

31 questions

Total time for this section: 45 Minutes

You can use a scientific calculator on this Section.

Reference Sheet

$A = \pi r^2$
$C = 2\pi r$

$A = \ell w$

$A = \dfrac{1}{2}bh$

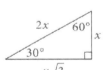
$c^2 = a^2 + b^2$

Special Right Triangles

$V = \ell w h$

$V = \pi r^2 h$

$V = \dfrac{4}{3}\pi r^3$

$V = \dfrac{1}{3}\pi r^2 h$

$V = \dfrac{1}{3}\ell w h$

The number of degrees of arc in a circle is 360.

The number of radians of arc in a circle is 2π.

The sum of the measures in degrees of the angles of a triangle is 180.

1) What is the value of $\frac{3a-2}{2}$, if $-2a + 4a + 6a = 48$?

A. 8

B. 6.5

C. 5.5

D. 5

2) What is the average (arithmetic mean) of all integers from 10 to 18?

A. 13

B. 14

C. 15

D. 15.5

3) What is the value of $|-13 - 6| - |-9 + 3|$?

A. 13

B. -13

C. 23

D. -23

4) The table represents different values of function $g(x)$. What is the value of $5g(-1) - 3g(2)$?

A. -12

B. -2

C. 3

D. 13

x	$g(x)$
-2	3
-1	2
0	1
1	0
2	-1
3	-2

5) A container holds 2.5 gallons of water when it is $\frac{5}{26}$ full. How many gallons of water does the container hold when it's full?

A. 8

B. 13

C. 17

D. 20

6) On the following figure, what is the area of the quadrilateral $ABCD$?

A. 22.5

B. 30

C. 33.2

D. 36

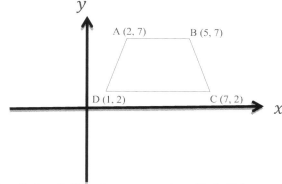

7) If n is an odd integer divisible by 3. Which of the following must be divisible by 2?

A. $n - 2$

B. $n + 2$

C. $2n + 2$

D. $2n - 1$

8) If $(3^a)^b = 243$, then what is the value of ab?

A. 2

B. 3

C. 4

D. 5

9) Multiply and write the product in scientific notation.

$$(2.9 \times 10^6) \times (2.6 \times 10^{-5})$$

A. 75.4×10^6

B. 75.4×10^{-5}

C. 7.54×10^{11}

D. 7.54×10

10) If the height of a right pyramid is $14\ cm$ and its base is a square with side $6\ cm$. What is its volume?

A. $432\ cm^3$

B. $236\ cm^3$

C. $172\ cm^3$

D. $168\ cm^3$

11) 5 less than twice a positive integer is 73. What is the integer?

A. 39

B. 41

C. 42

D. 44

12) What is the x-intercept of the line with equation $3x - 3y = 7$?

A. -7

B. -3

C. $\frac{7}{3}$

D. $\frac{5}{4}$

13) The perimeter of a triangle is 20 cm and the lengths of its sides are different integers. What is the greatest possible value of the biggest side?

A. 6 cm

B. 7 cm

C. 9 cm

D. 10 cm

14) If $(x - 2)^3 = 27$ which of the following could be the value of $(x - 6)(x - 4)$?

A. 1

B. 2

C. -2

D. -1

Questions 15 to 17 are based on the following data

A library has 840 books that include Mathematics, Physics, Chemistry, English and History.

Use following graph to answer questions 15 to 17.

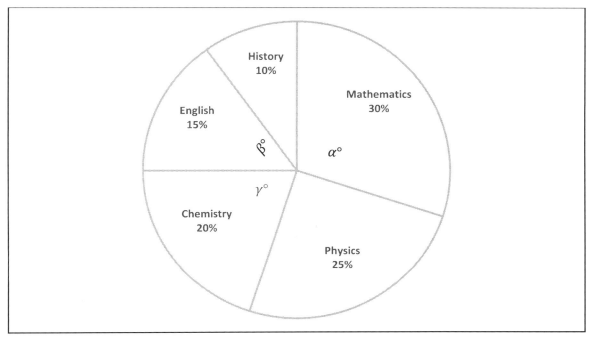

15) What is the product of the number of Mathematics and number of English books?

A. 21,168

B. 31,752

C. 26,460

D. 17,640

16) What are the values of angle α and β respectively?

A. $90°, 54°$

B. $120°, 36°$

C. $120°, 45°$

D. $108°, 54°$

17) The librarians decided to move some of the books in the Mathematics section to Chemistry section. How many books are in the Chemistry section if now $\gamma = \frac{2}{5}\alpha$?

A. 80

B. 120

C. 150

D. 180

18) In 1999, the average worker's income increased $3,000 per year starting from $25,000 annual salary. Which equation represents income greater than average? (I = income, x = number of years after 1999)

A. $I > 3,000\,x + 25,000$

B. $I > -3,000\,x + 25,000$

C. $I < -3,000\,x + 25,000$

D. $I < 3,000\,x - 25,000$

19) The Jackson Library is ordering some bookshelves. If x is the number of bookshelves the library wants to order, which each costs $200 and there is a one-time delivery charge of $900, which of the following represents the total cost, in dollar, per bookshelf?

A. $200x + 900$

B. $200 + 900x$

C. $\dfrac{200x+900}{200}$

D. $\dfrac{200x+900}{x}$

20) What is the sum of $\sqrt{x-9}$ and $\sqrt{x}-9$ when $\sqrt{x}=5$?

A. -3

B. -1

C. 0

D. 3

21) Given a right triangle $\triangle ABC$ whose $\angle B = 90°$, $\sin C = \frac{8}{17}$, find $\cos A$?

A. 1

B. $\frac{8}{15}$

C. $\frac{8}{17}$

D. $\frac{15}{17}$

22) In the following figure, AB is the diameter of the circle. What is the circumference of the circle?

A. 5π

B. 10π

C. 15π

D. 20π

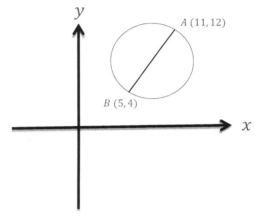

23) What is the smallest integer whose square root is greater than 7?

A. 9

B. 16

C. 25

D. 64

24) What is the area of the following equilateral triangle if the side $AB = 12\ cm$?

A. $36\sqrt{3}\ cm^2$

B. $18\sqrt{3}\ cm^2$

C. $6\sqrt{3}\ cm^2$

D. $8\ cm^2$

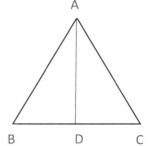

25) What is the solution of the following inequality?

$$|x - 3| \geq 4$$

A. $x \geq 7 \cup x \leq -1$

B. $-1 \leq x \leq 5$

C. $x \geq 5$

D. $x \leq -1$

26) If the area of the following rectangular $ABCD$ is 120, and E is the midpoint of AB, what is the area of the shaded part?

A. 25

B. 60

C. 75

D. 80

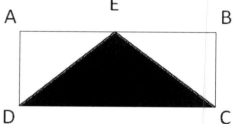

27) Which of the following is equivalent to $13 < -3x - 2 < 22$?

A. $-8 < x < -5$

B. $5 < x < 8$

C. $\frac{11}{3} < x < \frac{20}{3}$

D. $\frac{-20}{3} < x < \frac{-11}{3}$

Grid-ins Questions

Questions 28–31 are grid-ins questions. Solve the problems and enter your answers in the grid on the answer sheet as shown below.

Answer: 3.72

Answer: $\frac{6}{7}$

Write answers in the boxes

Grid in results

28) In five successive hours, a car traveled 40 km, 45 km, 50 km, 35 km and 55 km. In the next five hours, it traveled with an average speed of 65 $km\ per\ hour$. Find the total distance the car traveled in 10 hours.

29) If $\sin A = \frac{1}{5}$ in a right triangle and the angle A is an acute angle, then what is $\cos A$? (Round your answer to the nearest hundredths place).

30) 7 liters of water are poured into an aquarium that's $25cm$ long, $5cm$ wide, and $70cm$ high. How many cm will the water level in the aquarium rise due to this added water? (1 liter of water $= 1,000 \ cm^3$)?

31) If $x \begin{bmatrix} 3 & 0 \\ 0 & 4 \end{bmatrix} = \begin{bmatrix} x + 4y - 6 & 0 \\ 0 & 2y + 12 \end{bmatrix}$, what is the product of x and y?

STOP

This is the End of this Section. You may check your work on this section if you still have time.

PSAT Math Practice Test 2

2022 – 2023

Two Parts

Total number of questions: 48

Section 1 (No Calculator): 17 questions

Section 2 (Calculator): 31 questions

Total time for two parts: 70 Minutes

PSAT Practice Test 2 Answer Sheet

Remove (or photocopy) the answer sheets and use it to complete the practice tests.

PSAT Practice Test 2 – Section 1 Answer Sheet

1 Ⓐ Ⓑ Ⓒ Ⓓ   4 Ⓐ Ⓑ Ⓒ Ⓓ   7 Ⓐ Ⓑ Ⓒ Ⓓ   10 Ⓐ Ⓑ Ⓒ Ⓓ   13 Ⓐ Ⓑ Ⓒ Ⓓ

2 Ⓐ Ⓑ Ⓒ Ⓓ   5 Ⓐ Ⓑ Ⓒ Ⓓ   8 Ⓐ Ⓑ Ⓒ Ⓓ   11 Ⓐ Ⓑ Ⓒ Ⓓ

3 Ⓐ Ⓑ Ⓒ Ⓓ   6 Ⓐ Ⓑ Ⓒ Ⓓ   9 Ⓐ Ⓑ Ⓒ Ⓓ   12 Ⓐ Ⓑ Ⓒ Ⓓ

14   15   16   17

PSAT Practice Test 2 – Section 2 Answer Sheet

1 Ⓐ Ⓑ Ⓒ Ⓓ   7 Ⓐ Ⓑ Ⓒ Ⓓ   13 Ⓐ Ⓑ Ⓒ Ⓓ   19 Ⓐ Ⓑ Ⓒ Ⓓ   25 Ⓐ Ⓑ Ⓒ Ⓓ

2 Ⓐ Ⓑ Ⓒ Ⓓ   8 Ⓐ Ⓑ Ⓒ Ⓓ   14 Ⓐ Ⓑ Ⓒ Ⓓ   20 Ⓐ Ⓑ Ⓒ Ⓓ   26 Ⓐ Ⓑ Ⓒ Ⓓ

3 Ⓐ Ⓑ Ⓒ Ⓓ   9 Ⓐ Ⓑ Ⓒ Ⓓ   15 Ⓐ Ⓑ Ⓒ Ⓓ   21 Ⓐ Ⓑ Ⓒ Ⓓ   27 Ⓐ Ⓑ Ⓒ Ⓓ

4 Ⓐ Ⓑ Ⓒ Ⓓ   10 Ⓐ Ⓑ Ⓒ Ⓓ   16 Ⓐ Ⓑ Ⓒ Ⓓ   22 Ⓐ Ⓑ Ⓒ Ⓓ

5 Ⓐ Ⓑ Ⓒ Ⓓ   11 Ⓐ Ⓑ Ⓒ Ⓓ   17 Ⓐ Ⓑ Ⓒ Ⓓ   23 Ⓐ Ⓑ Ⓒ Ⓓ

6 Ⓐ Ⓑ Ⓒ Ⓓ   12 Ⓐ Ⓑ Ⓒ Ⓓ   18 Ⓐ Ⓑ Ⓒ Ⓓ   24 Ⓐ Ⓑ Ⓒ Ⓓ

28   **29**   **30**   **31**

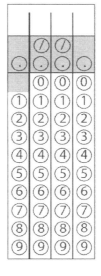

PSAT Mathematics Practice Test 2

Section 1

(No Calculator)

17 questions

Total time for this section: 25 Minutes

You may NOT use a calculator on this Section.

Reference Sheet

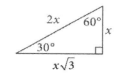

$A = \pi r^2$
$C = 2\pi r$

$A = \ell w$

$A = \frac{1}{2}bh$

$c^2 = a^2 + b^2$

Special Right Triangles

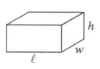

$V = \ell wh$

$V = \pi r^2 h$

$V = \frac{4}{3}\pi r^3$

$V = \frac{1}{3}\pi r^2 h$

$V = \frac{1}{3}\ell wh$

The number of degrees of arc in a circle is 360.

The number of radians of arc in a circle is 2π.

The sum of the measures in degrees of the angles of a triangle is 180.

1) A taxi driver earns $9 per 1-hour work. If he works 10 hours a day and in 1 hour he uses 2 −liters petrol with price $1 for 1-liter. How much money does he earn in one day?

A. $90

B. $88

C. $70

D. $60

2) Five years ago, Amy was three times as old as Mike was. If Mike is 10 years old now, how old is Amy?

A. 4

B. 8

C. 12

D. 20

3) What is the solution of the following system of equations?

$$\begin{cases} \dfrac{-x}{2} + \dfrac{y}{4} = 1 \\ \dfrac{-5y}{6} + 2x = 4 \end{cases}$$

A. $x = 48, y = 22$

B. $x = 50, y = 20$

C. $x = 20, y = 50$

D. $x = 22, y = 48$

4) What is the length of AB in the following figure if AE = 4, CD = 6 and AC = 12?

A. 3.8

B. 4.8

C. 7.2

D. 24

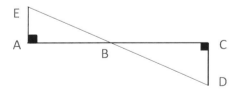

5) If a and b are solutions of the following equation, which of the following is the ratio $\frac{a}{b}$? ($a > b$)

$$2x^2 - 11x + 8 = -3x + 18$$

A. $\frac{1}{5}$

B. 5

C. $-\frac{1}{5}$

D. -5

6) How many tiles of $8\ cm^2$ is needed to cover a floor of dimension $6\ cm$ by $24\ cm$?

A. 6

B. 12

C. 18

D. 24

7) Which of the following is the solution of the following inequality?

$$2x + 4 > 11x - 12.5 - 3.5x$$

A. $x < 3$

B. $x > 3$

C. $x \leq 4$

D. $x \geq 4$

8) If a, b and c are positive integers and $3a = 4b = 5c$, then the value of $a + 2b + 15c$ is how many times the value of a?

A. 11.5

B. 12

C. 12.5

D. 15

9) A company pays its employer $7,000 plus 2% of all sales profit. If x is the number of all sales profit, which of the following represents the employer's revenue?

A. $0.02x$

B. $0.98x - 7,000$

C. $0.02x + 7,000$

D. $0.98x + 7,000$

10) If $f(x^2) = 3x + 4$, for all positive value of x, what is the value of $f(121)$?

A. 367

B. 37

C. 29

D. -29

11) $\frac{5x^2 + 75x - 80}{x^2 - 1}$?

A. $\frac{5x + 75}{x - 1}$

B. $\frac{x + 16}{x + 1}$

C. $\frac{5x + 80}{x + 1}$

D. $\frac{x + 15}{x - 1}$

12) If $x^2 + 6x - r$ is divisible by $(x - 5)$, what is the value of r?

A. 55

B. 56

C. 57

D. 58

13) If a parabola with equation $y = ax^2 + 5x + 10$, where a is constant passes through point $(2, 12)$, what is the value of a^2?

A. -2

B. 2

C. -4

D. 4

Grid-ins Questions

Questions 14–17 are grid-ins questions. Solve the problems and enter your answers in the grid on the answer sheet as shown below.

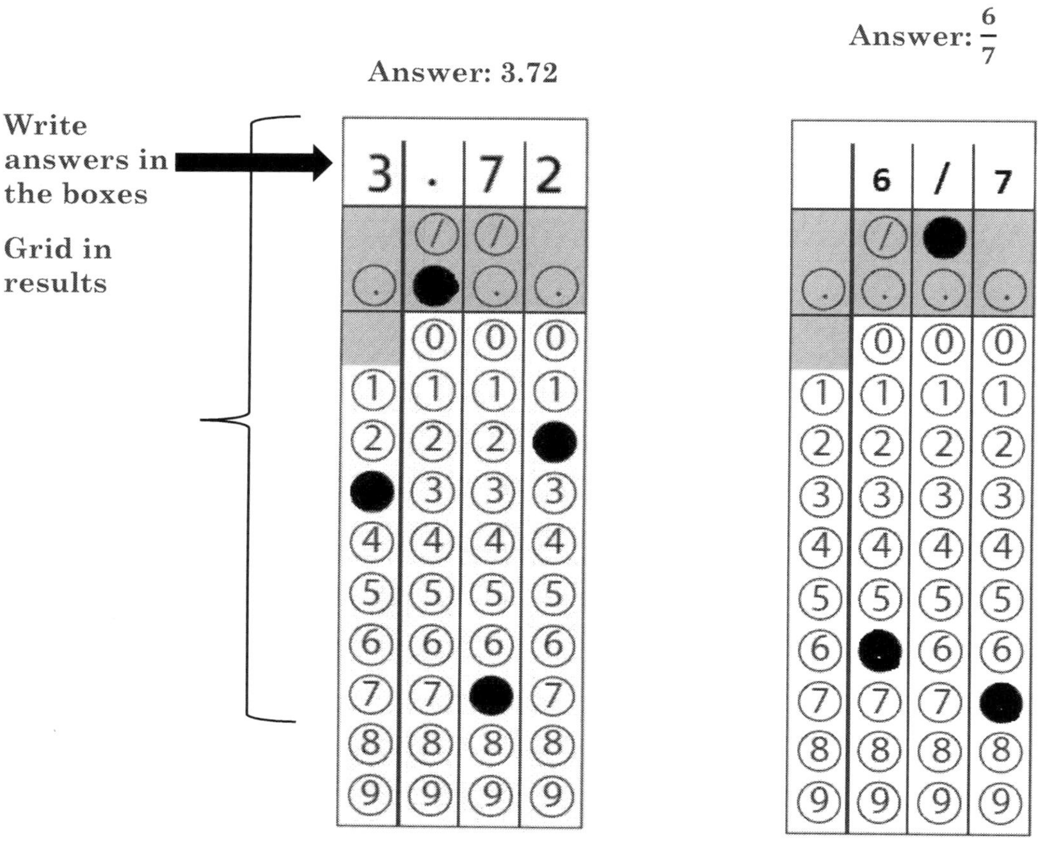

Answer: $\frac{6}{7}$

Answer: 3.72

Write answers in the boxes

Grid in results

14) In the following equation, what is the value of $y - 3x$?

$$\frac{y}{5} = x - \frac{2}{5}x + 10$$

15) What is the value of x in the following equation?

$$\frac{x^2 - 9}{x + 3} + 2(x + 4) = 15$$

16) If $x \neq 0$, what is the value of $\frac{(10(x)(y^2))^2}{(8xy^2)^2}$?

17) What is the slope of a line containing the reflected points of $A(2, -1)$ and $B(1, 3)$ over the line $y = x$?

STOP

This is the End of this Section. You may check your work on this section if you still have time.

PSAT Mathematics Practice Test 2

Section 2
(Calculator)

31 questions

Total time for this section: 45 Minutes

You can use a scientific calculator on this Section.

Reference Sheet

$A = \pi r^2$
$C = 2\pi r$

$A = \ell w$

$A = \dfrac{1}{2}bh$

$c^2 = a^2 + b^2$

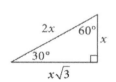

Special Right Triangles

$V = \ell w h$

$V = \pi r^2 h$

$V = \dfrac{4}{3}\pi r^3$

$V = \dfrac{1}{3}\pi r^2 h$

$V = \dfrac{1}{3}\ell w h$

The number of degrees of arc in a circle is 360.

The number of radians of arc in a circle is 2π.

The sum of the measures in degrees of the angles of a triangle is 180.

1) If a car has 80-liter petrol and after one hour driving the car use 6-liter petrol, how much petrol will remain after x-hours driving?

A. $6x - 80$

B. $80 + 6x$

C. $80 - 6x$

D. $80 - x$

2) 12 less than three times a positive integer is 120. What is the integer?

A. 39

B. 41

C. 42

D. 44

3) The following graph shows the mark of six students in mathematics. What is the mean (average) of the marks?

A. 15

B. 14.5

C. 14

D. 13.5

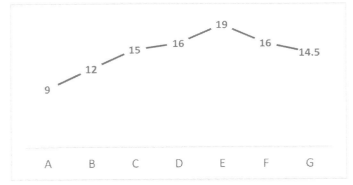

4) The area of a circle is 64π. What is the circumference of the circle?

A. 8π

B. 16π

C. 32π

D. 64π

5) Which of the following values for x and y satisfy the following system of equations?

$$\begin{cases} x + 4y = 10 \\ 5x + 10y = 20 \end{cases}$$

A. $x = 3, y = 2$

B. $x = 2, y - 3$

C. $x = -2, y = 3$

D. $x = 3, y = -2$

6) If $a \neq 0$ and $6b = 5a\sqrt{3}$, then what is the value of $\frac{2b\sqrt{3}}{4a}$?

A. $\frac{5}{4}$

B. $\frac{5}{4}a$

C. $2a$

D. $2a\sqrt{3}$

7) If a gas tank can hold 25 gallons, how many gallons does it contain when it is $\frac{2}{5}$ full?

A. 50

B. 125

C. 62.5

D. 10

8) In the xy-plane, the point $(4, 3)$ and $(3, 2)$ are on line A. Which of the following equations of lines is parallel to line A?

A. $y = 3x$

B. $y = \frac{x}{2}$

C. $y = 2x$

D. $y = x$

9) In the following graph, which of the data point is farthest from the line of best fit (not shown)?

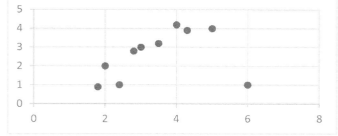

A. $(6, 1)$

B. $(5, 4)$

C. $(3, 3)$

D. $(2, 2)$

10) A football team won exactly 80% of the games it played during last session. Which of the following could be the total number of games the team played last season?

A. 49

B. 35

C. 12

D. 32

11) If x is greater than 0 and less than 1, which of the following is true?

A. $x < \sqrt{x^2 + 1} < \sqrt{x^2} + 1$

B. $x < \sqrt{x^2 + 1} < \sqrt{x^2 + 1}$

C. $\sqrt{x^2 + 1} < x < \sqrt{x^2} + 1$

D. $\sqrt{x^2} + 1 < \sqrt{x^2 + 1} < x$

12) If x is directly proportional to the square of y, and $y = 2$ when $x = 12$, then when $x = 75$ $y = ?$

A. $\frac{1}{5}$

B. 1

C. 5

D. 25

13) Jack earns $616 for his first 44 hours of work in a week and is then paid 1.5 times his regular hourly rate for any additional hours. This week, Jack needs $826 to pay his rent, bills and other expenses. How many hours must he work to make enough money in this week?

A. 40

B. 48

C. 53

D. 54

Questions 14 and 16 are based on the following data

Types of air pollutions in 10 cities of a country

Type of Pollution	Number of Cities									
A										
B										
C										
D										
E										
	1	2	3	4	5	6	7	8	9	10

14) If a is the mean (average) of the number of cities in each pollution type category, b is the mode, and c is the median of the number of cities in each pollution type category, then which of the following must be true?

A. $a < b < c$

B. $b < a < c$

C. $a = c$

D. $b < c = a$

15) What percent of cities are in the type of pollution A, C, and D respectively?

A. 60%, 40%, 90%

B. 30%, 40%, 90%

C. 30%, 40%, 60%

D. 40%, 60%, 90%

16) How many cities should be added to type of pollutions B until the ratio of cities in type of pollution B to cities in type of pollution E will be 0.625?

A. 2

B. 3

C. 4

D. 5

17) The ratio of boys and girls in a class is $4 : 7$. If there are 44 students in the class, how many more boys should be enrolled to make the ratio $1 : 1$?

A. 8

B. 10

C. 12

D. 16

18) In the following right triangle, if the sides AB and AC become twice longer, what will be the ratio of the perimeter of the triangle to its area?

A. $\frac{1}{2}$

B. 2

C. $\frac{1}{3}$

D. 3

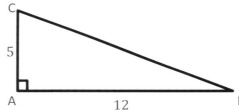

19) The capacity of a red box is 20% bigger than the capacity of a blue box. If the red box can hold 30 equal sized books, how many of the same books can the blue box hold?

A. 9

B. 15

C. 21

D. 25

20) The sum of six different negative integers is -70. If the smallest of these integers is -15, what is the largest possible value of one of the other five integers?

A. -14

B. -10

C. -5

D. -1

21) What is the ratio of the minimum value to the maximum value of the following function?

$$-2 \le x \le 3? \quad f(x) = -3x + 1$$

A. $\frac{7}{8}$

B. $-\frac{8}{7}$

C. $-\frac{7}{8}$

D. $\frac{8}{7}$

Questions 22 to 24 are based on the following data

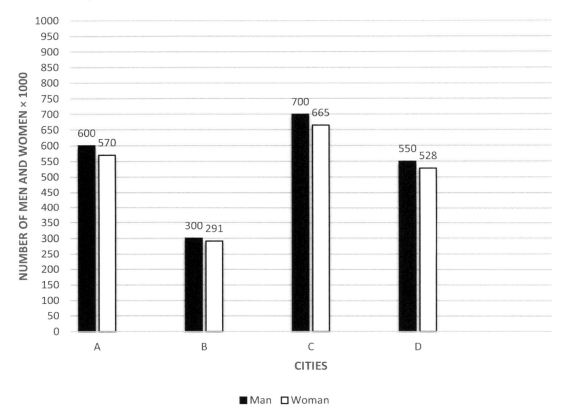

22) What's the maximum ratio of woman to man in the four cities?

A. 0.98

B. 0.97

C. 0.96

D. 0.95

23) What's the ratio of percentage of men in city A to percentage of women in city C?

A. 0.9

B. 0.95

C. 1

D. 1.05

24) How many women should be added to city D until the ratio of women to men will be 1.2?

A. 120

B. 128

C. 132

D. 160

25) In the rectangle below if $y > 5\ cm$ and the area of rectangle is $50\ cm^2$ and the perimeter of the rectangle is $30\ cm$, what is the value of x and y respectively?

A. $4, 11$

B. $5, 11$

C. $5, 10$

D. $4, 10$

26) Given the right triangle bellow, $sin\ (\beta)$ is equal to?

A. $\frac{a}{b}$

B. $\frac{a}{\sqrt{a^2+b^2}}$

C. $\frac{\sqrt{a^2+b^2}}{ab}$

D. $\frac{b}{\sqrt{a^2+b^2}}$

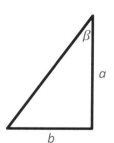

27) Solve the following inequality.

$$\left|\frac{x}{2} - 2x + 10\right| < 5$$

A. $-\frac{10}{3} < x < 10$

B. $-10 < x < \frac{10}{3}$

C. $\frac{10}{3} < x < 10$

D. $-10 < x < -\frac{10}{3}$

Grid-ins Questions

Questions 28–31 are grid-ins questions. Solve the problems and enter your answers in the grid on the answer sheet as shown below.

Answer: 3.72

Answer: $\dfrac{6}{7}$

Write answers in the boxes

Grid in results

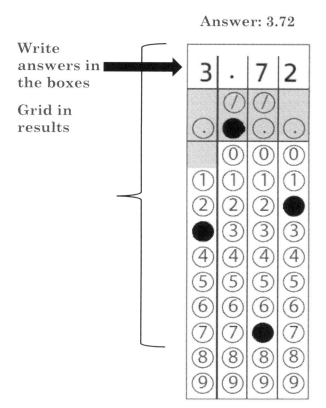

28) $f(x) = ax^2 + bx + c$ is a quadratic function where a, b and c are constant. The value of x of the point of intersection of this quadratic function and linear function $g(x) = 2x - 3$ is 2. The vertex of $f(x)$ is at $(-2, 5)$. What is the product of a, b and c?

29) A ladder leans against a wall forming a 60° angle between the ground and the ladder. If the bottom of the ladder is 30 feet away from the wall, how many feet is the ladder?

30) The volume of cube A is $\frac{1}{2}$ of its surface area. What is the length of an edge of cube A?

31) If $3x + 6y = \frac{-3y^2 + 15}{x}$, what is the value of $(x + y)^2$? $(x \neq 0)$

STOP

This is the End of this Section. You may check your work on this section if you still have time.

PSAT Math Practice Tests Answers and Explanations

Now, it's time to review your results to see where you went wrong and what areas you need to improve!

PSAT Math Practice Test 1					PSAT Math Practice Test 2				
Section 1		**Section 2**			**Section 1**		**Section 2**		
1	A	1	A	21	C	1	C	1	C	21	B
2	B	2	B	22	B	2	D	2	D	22	B
3	D	3	A	23	D	3	D	3	B	23	D
4	D	4	D	24	A	4	B	4	B	24	C
5	D	5	B	25	A	5	D	5	C	25	C
6	C	6	A	26	B	6	C	6	A	26	D
7	C	7	C	27	A	7	A	7	D	27	C
8	D	8	D	28	550	8	A	8	D	28	1
9	C	9	D	29	0.94	9	C	9	A	29	60
10	C	10	D	30	80	10	B	10	B	30	3
11	B	11	A	31	20	11	C	11	A	31	3
12	B	12	C			12	A	12	C		
13	D	13	C			13	D	13	D		
14	200	14	D			14	50	14	C		
15	90	15	B			15	10/3	15	A		
16	456	16	D			16	25/16	16	A		
17	3.5	17	B			17	−1/4	17	C		
		18	A					18	A		
		19	C					19	D		
		20	C					20	C		

How to score your test

PSAT/ NMSQT scores are broken down by three sections: Math, Reading, and Writing.

For the Math and Reading, the score scale is 160 - 760 for a total of 1520 possible points on the PSAT. The total scaled score for PSAT test is the sum of the scores for these two sections. The scaled score is converted from the raw score a student earns on each section. The Writing section has a score range of 0-6, in half-point increments, and it is provided separately.

Students will also receive a percentile score of between 1-99% that compares their test scores with other test takers.

To find your score on the practice tests on this book, your raw score has to be converted to a scaled score (the official score you receive). Your raw score is the number of points you earned on the exam (you get a point for each question you answer correctly, and no points are deducted for incorrect answers).

To figure out your PSAT Math Practice Test scores, follow the following steps:

1. Find your raw score on each of the two math sections (No Calculator and Calculator sections). This is the total number of questions you answered correctly.

2. Add your raw scores in the two Math sections: No-Calculator raw score and Calculator raw score

3. Use the next table to convert your raw score to scaled score.

	PSAT/ NMSQT Math Scaled Scores									
Raw Score	Scaled Score	Raw Score	Scaled Score	Raw Score	Scaled Score	Raw Score	Scaled Score	Raw Score	Scaled Score
0	160	11	400	22	530	33	630	44	740
1	190	12	420	23	540	34	640	45	750
2	210	13	430	24	550	35	650	46	750
3	240	14	440	25	560	36	660	47	760
4	270	15	460	26	560	37	680	48	760
5	290	16	470	27	570	38	690		
6	320	17	480	28	580	39	710		
7	340	18	490	29	590	40	720		
8	360	19	500	30	600	41	730		
9	370	20	510	31	610	42	730		
10	390	21	520	32	620	43	740		

PSAT Math Practice Test 1: Section 1

1) Choice A is correct

$5x - 8 = 4.5 \rightarrow 5x = 4.5 + 8 = 12.5 \rightarrow x = \frac{12.5}{3} = 2.5$

Then; $3x + 3 = 3(2.5) + 3 = 7.5 + 3 = 10.5$

2) Choice B is correct

$f(x) = x^2 + 2x - 10, f(4t^2) = (4t^2)^2 + 2(4t^2) - 5 = 16t^4 + 8t^2 - 10$

3) Choice D is correct

$xp + 2yq = 27 \rightarrow xp = 27 - 2yq$. Substitute the value of xp in the second equation. Then:

$(27 - 2yq) + yq = 18 \rightarrow 27 - yq = 18 \rightarrow yq = 27 - 18 = 9$

4) Choice D is correct

Let x be all expenses, then $\frac{22}{100}x = \$770 \rightarrow x = \frac{100 \times \$770}{22} = \$3,500$

Nicole spent for her rent: $\frac{27}{100} \times \$3,500 = \$945$

5) Choice D is correct

Two factors of the polynomial $30a^4 + b$ are provided. Let x be another factor of the polynomial. Then:

$30a^2 + b = x(a^2 + 6)(a^2 - 6) = xa^4 - 36x \rightarrow x = 30$ And

$$b = -36a = -36 \times 30 = -1080$$

6) Choice C is correct

$\frac{3}{8} = 0.375 \rightarrow C = 5, \frac{2}{25} = 0.08 \rightarrow D = 8 \rightarrow C \times D = 5 \times 8 = 40$

7) Choice C is correct

y is the intersection of the three circles. Therefore, it must be even (from circle A), negative (from circle B), and multiple of 6 (from circle C). From the choice, only -6 is even, negative and multiple of 6.

8) Choice D is correct

let x be total number of cards in the box, then number of red cards is: $x - 246$

The probability of choosing a red card is one third. Then: $probability = \frac{1}{3} = \frac{x-132}{x}$

Use cross multiplication to solve for x. $x \times 1 = 3(x - 246) \rightarrow x = 3x - 738 \rightarrow 2x = 738 \rightarrow x = 369$.

9) Choice C is correct

Plug in the values of x in each equation and check.

I. $(-2)^2 - 3(-2) - 25 = 4 + 6 - 25 = -15 \neq 0$

$(5)^2 - 3(5) - 25 = 25 - 15 - 25 = -15 \neq 0$

II. $2(-2)^2 - 6(-2) = 8 + 12 = 20 \rightarrow 20 = 20$

$2(5)^2 - 6(5) = 50 - 30 = 20 \rightarrow 20 = 20$

III. $4(-2)^2 - 12(-2) - 40 = 16 + 24 - 40 = 0$

$4(5)^2 - 12(5) - 40 = 100 - 60 - 40 = 0$

Equations II and III are correct.

10) Choice C is correct

Let P be circumference of circle A, then; $2\pi r_A = 24\pi \rightarrow r_A = 12$, $r_A = 3r_B \rightarrow r_B = \frac{12}{3} = 4 \rightarrow$ Area of circle B is; $\pi r_B^2 = 16\pi$

11) Choice B is correct

Number of biology book: 30, Total number of books; $30 + 90 + 60 = 210$

the ratio of the number of biology books to the total number of books is: $\frac{30}{180} = \frac{1}{6}$

12) Choice B is correct

Let's find the angles α and β.

$\alpha = 180° - 118° = 62°$

$\beta = 180° - 145° = 35°$

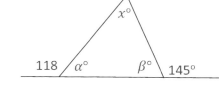

All angles in a triangle sum up to 180 degrees. Then:

$x + \alpha + \beta = 180° \rightarrow x = 180° - 62° - 35° = 83°$

13) Choice D is correct

A. $f(x) = x^2 - 5$ if $x = 1 \rightarrow f(1) = (1)^2 - 5 = 1 - 5 = -4 \neq 4$

B. $f(x) = x^2 - 1$ if $x = 1 \rightarrow f(1) = (1)^2 - 1 = 1 - 1 = 0 \neq 4$

C. $f(x) = \sqrt{x + 2}$ if $x = 1 \rightarrow f(1) = \sqrt{1 + 2} = \sqrt{3} \neq 4$

D. $f(x) = \sqrt{x} + 3$ if $x = 1 \rightarrow f(1) = \sqrt{1} + 3 = 4$

$f(4) = \sqrt{4} + 3 = 7$, $f(9) = \sqrt{9} + 3 = 6$, $f(16) = \sqrt{16} + 3 = 7$

Choice D is correct.

14) The answer is 200

Let a be the amount of time Mia can do the job and Let b be the amount of time Moe can do the job. Then: $\frac{1}{5} + \frac{1}{b} = \frac{1}{2} \rightarrow \frac{1}{5} + \frac{1}{b} = \frac{1}{2} \rightarrow \frac{1}{b} = \frac{1}{2} - \frac{1}{5} = \frac{3}{10} \rightarrow b = \frac{10}{3} = 3\frac{1}{3}$

Then: $b = 3\frac{1}{3} \times 60 = 200$ minutes

15) The answer is 90

In the equilateral triangle if x is length of one side of triangle, then the perimeter of the triangle is $3x$. Then $3x = 45 \rightarrow x = 15$ and radius of the circle is: $x = 15$, Then, the perimeter of the circle is: $2\pi r = 2\pi(15) = 30\pi$, $\pi = 3 \rightarrow 30\pi = 30 \times 3 = 90$

16) The answer is 456

$\frac{14}{100}x = 84 \rightarrow x = \frac{84 \times 100}{14} = 600$, $\frac{1}{8}y = 18 \rightarrow y = 8 \times 18 = 144$

$\rightarrow x - y = 600 - 144 = 456$

17) The answer is 3.5 or $3\frac{1}{2}$

One degree equals $\frac{\pi}{180}$. The angle α in radians is equal to the angle α in degrees times π constant divided by 180 degrees. Then: $1\ degree = \frac{\pi}{180} \rightarrow 630\ degrees = \frac{630\pi}{180} = 3.5\pi$, $3.5\pi = x\pi \rightarrow x = 3.5$

PSAT Math Practice Test 1: Section 2

1) Choice A is correct

$-2a + 4a + 6a = 48 \to 8a = 48 \to a = \frac{48}{8} = 6$, sThen; $\frac{3a-2}{2} = \frac{3(6)-2}{2} = \frac{18-2}{2} = 8$

2) Choice B is correct

All integers from 10 to 18 are: $10, 11, 12, 13, 14, 15, 16, 17, 18$

The mean of these integers is: $\frac{10+11+12+13+14+15+16+17+18}{9} = \frac{126}{9} = 14$

3) Choice A is correct

$|-13 - 6| - |-9 + 3| = |-19| - |-6| = 19 - 6 = 13$

4) Choice D is correct

Based on the table provided:

$g(-2) = g(x = -2) = 3$, $g(3) = g(x = 3) = -2$, $3g(-2) - 2g(3) = 3(3) - 2(-2) = 9 + 4 = 13$

5) Choice B is correct

let x be the number of gallons of water the container holds when it is full.

Then; $\frac{5}{26}x = 2.5 \to x = \frac{26 \times 2.5}{5} = 13$

6) Choice A is correct

The quadrilateral is a trapezoid. Use the formula of the area of trapezoids. $Area = \frac{1}{2}h(b_1 + b_2)$

You can find the height of the trapezoid by finding the difference of the values of y for the points A and D. (or points B and C). You can also find the distance of A and B by finding the difference of the values of x for the points A and B. Use same method to find the distance of D and C. $h = 8 - 2 = 5$, $AB = 5 - 2 = 3$, $CD = 7 - 1 = 6$

Area of the trapezoid is: $\frac{1}{2}h(b_1 + b_2) = \frac{1}{2}(5)(3 + 6) = 22.5$

7) Choice C is correct

Choose a random number for n and check the options. Let n be equal to 9 which is divisible by 3, then:

A. $n - 2 = 9 - 2 = 7$ is not divisible by 2

B. $n + 2 = 9 + 2 = 11$ is not divisible by 2

C. $2n + 2 = 2 \times 9 = 188$ is divisible by 2. Try 15, 21, … . For all values of n, $2n + 2$ is divisible by 2.

D. $2n - 1 = (2 \times 9) - 1 = 17$ is not divisible by 2.

8) Choice D is correct

$(3^a)^b = 243 \rightarrow 3^{ab} = 243, 81 = 3^5 \rightarrow 3^{ab} = 3^5, \rightarrow ab = 5$

9) Choice D is correct

$(2.9 \times 10^6) \times (2.6 \times 10^{-5}) = (2.9 \times 2.6) \times (10^6 \times 10^{-5}) = 7.54 \times (10^{6+(-5)}) = 7.54 \times 10^1$

10) Choice D is correct

The formula of the volume of pyramid is: $V = \frac{l \times w \times h}{3}$

The length and width of the pyramid is $6 \ cm$ and its height is $14 \ cm$. Therefore:

$V = \frac{6 \times 6 \times 14}{3} = 168 \ cm^3$

11) Choice A is correct

Let x be the integer. Then: $2x - 5 = 73$, Add 5 both sides: $2x = 78$, Divide both sides by 2: $x = 39$

12) Choice C is correct

The value of y in the x-intercept of a line is zero. Then: $y = 0 \rightarrow 3x - 3(0) = 7 \rightarrow 3x = 7 \rightarrow x = \frac{7}{3}$, then, x-intercept of the line is $\frac{7}{3}$.

13) Choice C is correct

The sum of the lengths of any two sides of triangle is greater than the length of the third side, therefore the greatest possible value of the biggest side equal to $9 \ cm. \ 9 < 11$

14) Choice D is correct

$(x - 2)^3 = 27 \rightarrow$ Find the third root of both sides. Then: $x - 2 = 3 \rightarrow x = 5$

$\rightarrow (x - 6)(x - 4) = (5 - 6)(6 - 4) = (-1)(2) = -2$

15) Choice B is correct

Number of Mathematics books: $0.3 \times 840 = 252$

Number of English books: $0.15 \times 840 = 126$

Product of number of Mathematics and number of English books: $252 \times 126 = 31,752$

16) Choice D is correct

The angle α is: $0.3 \times 360 = 108°$

The angle β is: $0.15 \times 360 = 54°$

17) Choice B is correct

According to the chart, 50% of the books are in the Mathematics and Chemistry sections.

Therefore, there are 420 books in these two sections. $0.50 \times 840 = 420$

$\gamma + \alpha = 420$, and $\gamma = \frac{2}{5}\alpha$, Replace γ by $\frac{2}{5}\alpha$ in the first equation.

$\gamma + \alpha = 420 \rightarrow \frac{2}{5}\alpha + \alpha = 420 \rightarrow \frac{7}{5}\alpha = 420 \rightarrow multiply\ both\ sides\ by\ \frac{5}{7}$

$\left(\frac{5}{7}\right)\frac{7}{5}\alpha = 420 \times \left(\frac{5}{7}\right) \rightarrow \alpha = \frac{420 \times 5}{7} = 300,\ \alpha = 300 \rightarrow \gamma = \frac{2}{5}\alpha \rightarrow \gamma = \frac{2}{5} \times 300 = 120$

There are 120 books in the Chemistry section.

18) Choice A is correct

Let x be the number of years. Therefore, \$3,000 per year equals $3,000x$. Starting from \$25,000 annual salary means you should add that amount to $3,000x$. Income more than that is: $I > 3,000\ x + 25,000$

19) Choice C is correct

The amount of money for x bookshelf is: $200x$, Then, the total cost of all bookshelves is equal to: $100x + 800$, The total cost, in dollar, per bookshelf is: $\frac{Total\ cost}{number\ of\ items} = \frac{200x + 900}{x}$

20) Choice C is correct

$\sqrt{x} = 5 \rightarrow x = 25$, then; $\sqrt{x} - 9 = \sqrt{25} - 9 = 5 - 9 = -4$ and $\sqrt{x-9} = \sqrt{25-9} = \sqrt{16} = 4$

Then: $\left(\sqrt{x-9}\right) + \left(\sqrt{x} - 9\right) = 4 + (-4) = 0$

21) Choice C is correct

To solve for $\cos A$ first identify what is known. The question states that ΔABC is a right triangle whose $\angle B = 90°$ and $\sin C = \frac{8}{17}$.

It is important to recall that any triangle has a sum of interior angles that equals 180 degrees. Therefore, to calculate $\cos A$ use the complimentary angles identify of trigonometric function. $\cos A = \cos(90 - C)$, Then: $\cos A = \sin C$

For complementary angles, sin of one angle is equal to cos of the other angle. $\cos A = \frac{8}{17}$

22) Choice B is correct

The distance of A to B on the coordinate plane is: $\sqrt{(x_1 - x_2)^2 + (y_1 - y_2)^2} = \sqrt{(11 - 5)^2 + (12 - 4)^2} = \sqrt{6^2 + 8^2}, = \sqrt{36 + 64} = \sqrt{100} = 10$

The diameter of the circle is 10 and the radius of the circle is 5. Then: the circumference of the circle is: $2\pi r = 2\pi(5) = 10\pi$

23) Choice D is correct

Square root of 9 is $\sqrt{9} = 3 < 7$, Square root of 16 is $\sqrt{16} = 4 < 7$, Square root of 25 is $\sqrt{5} = 5 < 7$, Square root of 64 is $\sqrt{64} = 8 > 7$, then the answer is C.

24) Choice A is correct

Area of the triangle is: $\frac{1}{2} AD \times BC$ and AD is perpendicular to BC. Triangle ADC is a

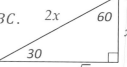

$30° - 60° - 90°$ right triangle. The relationship among all sides of right triangle $30° - 60° - 90°$ is provided in the following triangle: In this triangle, the opposite side of $30°$ angle is half of the hypotenuse. And the opposite side of $60°$ is opposite of $30° \times \sqrt{3}$

$CD = 6$, then $AD = 6 \times \sqrt{3}$

Area of the triangle ABC is: $\frac{1}{2} AD \times BC = \frac{1}{2} 6\sqrt{3} \times 12 = 36\sqrt{3}$

25) Choice A is correct

$|x - 3| \geq 4$. Then: $x - 3 \geq 4 \rightarrow x \geq 3 + 4 \rightarrow x \geq 7$, Or $x - 3 \leq -4 \rightarrow x \leq -4 + 3 \rightarrow x \leq -1$. Then, the solution is: $x \geq 7 \cup x \leq -1$

26) Choice B is correct

Since, E is the midpoint of AB, then the area of all triangles DAE, DEF, CFE and CBE are equal.

Let x be the area of one of the triangle, Then: $4x = 120 \rightarrow x = 30$

The area of DEC $= 2x = 2(30) = 60$

27) Choice A is correct

$13 < -3x - 2 < 22 \rightarrow$ Add 2 to all sides.

$13 + 2 < -3x - 2 + 2 < 22 + 2$

$\rightarrow 15 < -3x < 24 \rightarrow$ Divide all sides by -3. (Remember that when you divide all sides of an inequality by a negative number, the inequality sing will be swapped. $<$ becomes $>$)

$\frac{15}{-3} > \frac{-3x}{-3} > \frac{24}{-3}, \quad -8 < x < -5$

28) The answer is 550

Add the first 5 numbers. $40 + 45 + 50 + 35 + 55 = 225$, To find the distance traveled in the next 5 hours, multiply the average by number of hours.

$Distance = Average \times Rate = 65 \times 5 = 325$. Add both numbers. $325 + 225 = 550$

29) The answer is 0.94

$\sin(A) = \frac{opposite}{hypotenuse} = \frac{1}{3} \Rightarrow$ We have the following triangle, then:

$c = \sqrt{3^2 - 1^2} = \sqrt{9 - 1} = \sqrt{8}$

$\cos(A) = \frac{\sqrt{8}}{3}$

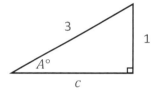

Rounding the answer to the nearest hundredths, gives 0.94

30) The answer is 80

$One\ liter = 1,000\ cm^3 \rightarrow 6\ liters = 6,000\ cm^3$

$6,000 = 15 \times 5 \times h \rightarrow h = \frac{6,000}{75} = 80\ cm$

31) The answer is 20

Based on corresponding members of each matrix, write two equations:

$\begin{cases} 3x = x + 4y - 6 \\ 4x = 2y + 12 \end{cases} \rightarrow \begin{cases} 2x - 4y = -6 \\ 4x - 2y = 12 \end{cases}$ Multiply first equation by (-2), then

$\begin{cases} -4x + 8y = 12 \\ 4x - 2y = 12 \end{cases}$ Add two equations:

$\rightarrow 6y = 24 \rightarrow y = 4 \rightarrow x = 5 \rightarrow x \times y = 20$

PSAT Math Practice Test 2: Section 1

1) Choice C is correct

$9 \times 10 = \$90$, Petrol use: $10 \times 2 = 20$ liters, Petrol cost: $20 \times \$1 = \$20$

Money earned: $\$90 - \$20 = \$70$

2) Choice D is correct

Five years ago, Amy was three times as old as Mike. Mike is 10 years now. Therefore, 5 years ago Mike was 5 years. Five years ago, Amy was: $A = 3 \times 5 = 15$, Now Amy is 20 years old: $15 + 5 = 20$

3) Choice D is correct

$\begin{cases} \frac{-x}{2} + \frac{y}{4} = 1 \\ \frac{-5y}{6} + 2x = 4 \end{cases}$ → Multiply the top equation by 4. Then,

$\begin{cases} -2x + y = 4 \\ \frac{-5y}{6} + 2x = 4 \end{cases}$ → Add two equations.

$\frac{1}{6}y = 8 \to y = 48$, plug in the value of y into the first equation $\to x = 22$

4) Choice B is correct

Two triangles ΔBAE and ΔBCD are similar. Then:

$\frac{AE}{CD} = \frac{AB}{BC} \to \frac{4}{6} = \frac{x}{12} \to 48 - 4x = 6x \to 10x = 48 \to x = 4.8$

5) Choice D is correct

$2x^2 - 11x + 8 = -3x + 18 \to 2x^2 - 11x + 3x + 8 - 18 = 0 \to 2x^2 - 8x - 10 = 0$

$\to 2(x^2 - 4x - 5) = 0 \to$ Divide both sides by 2. Then: $x^2 - 4x - 5 = 0$, Find the factors of the quadratic equation. $\to (x - 5)(x + 1) = 0 \to x = 5$ or $x = -1$

$a > b$, then: $a = 5$ and $b = -1$, $\frac{a}{b} = \frac{5}{-1} = -5$

6) Choice C is correct

The area of the floor is: $6 \, cm \times 24 \, cm = 144 \, cm^2$, The number is tiles needed $= 144 \div 8 = 18$

7) Choice A is correct

$2x + 4 > 11x - 12.5 - 3.5x \to$ Combine like terms:

$2x + 4 > 7.5x - 12.5 \to$ Subtract $2x$ from both sides: $4 > 5.5x - 12.5$

Add 12.5 both sides of the inequality. $16.5 > 5.5x$, Divide both sides by 5.5. $\frac{16.5}{5.5} > x \to x < 3$

8) Choice A is correct

$3a = 4b \rightarrow b = \frac{3a}{4}$ and $3a = 5c \rightarrow c = \frac{3a}{5}$

$a + 2b + 15c = a + \left(2 \times \dfrac{3a}{4}\right) + \left(15 \times \dfrac{3a}{5}\right) = a + 1.5a + 9a = 11.5a$

9) Choice C is correct

x is the number of all sales profit and 2% of it is: $2\% \times x = 0.02x$, Employer's revenue:

$0.2x + 7,000$

10) Choice B is correct

$x^2 = 121 \rightarrow x = 11$ (positive value) Or $x = -11$ (negative value)

Since x is positive, then: $f(121) = f(11^2) = 3(11) + 4 = 33 + 4 = 37$

11) Choice C is correct

First, find the factors of numerator and denominator of the expression. Then simplify.

$\dfrac{5x^2+75x-80}{x^2-1} = \dfrac{5(x^2+15x-16)}{(x-1)(x+1)} = \dfrac{5(x+16)(x-1)}{(x-1)(x+1)} = \dfrac{5(x+16)}{(x+1)} = \dfrac{5x+80}{x+1}$

12) Choice A is correct

If $r = 55 \rightarrow \dfrac{x^2+6x-55}{x-5} = \dfrac{(x+11)(x-5)}{(x-5)} = x + 11$, For all other options, the numerator expression is not divisible by $(x - 5)$.

13) Choice D is correct

Plug in the values of x and y in the equation of the parabola. Then:

$12 = a(2)^2 + 5(2) + 10 \rightarrow 12 = 4a + 10 + 10 \rightarrow 12 = 4a + 20$

$\rightarrow 4a = 12 - 20 = -8 \rightarrow a = \dfrac{-8}{4} = -2 \rightarrow a^2 = (-2)^2 = 4$

14) The answer is 50

$\dfrac{y}{5} = x - \dfrac{2}{5}x + 10$, Multiply both sides of the equation by 5. Then:

$5 \times \dfrac{y}{5} = 5 \times \left(x - \dfrac{2}{5}x + 10\right) \rightarrow y = 5x - 2x + 50 \rightarrow y = 3x + 50$

Now, subtract $3x$ from both sides of the equation. Then: $y - 3x = 50$

15) The answer is $\frac{10}{3}$.

First, factorize the numerator and simplify.

$\frac{x^2-9}{x+3} + 2(x+4) = 15 \rightarrow \frac{(x-3)(x+3)}{x+3} + 2x + 8 = 15, \rightarrow x - 3 + 2x + 8 = 15 \rightarrow 3x + 5 = 15$

Subtract 5 from both sides of the equation. Then: $\rightarrow 3x = 15 - 5 = 10 \rightarrow x = \frac{10}{3}$

16) The answer is $\frac{25}{16}$.

First, simplify the numerator and the denominator. $\frac{(10(x)(y^2)^2}{(8xy^2)^2} = \frac{100x^2y^4}{64x^2y^4}$

Remove x^2y^4 from both numerator and denominator. $\frac{100x^2y^4}{64x^2y^4} = \frac{100}{64} = \frac{25}{16}$

17) The answer is $-\frac{1}{4}$ or -0.25

Remember that, the reflection of the point (x, y) over the line $y = x$ is the point (y, x). Then:

The reflected point of $A(2, -1)$, is $(-1, 2)$, The reflected point of $B(1, 3)$ is point $(3, 1)$

Therefore, the slope of the reflected line is: $m = \frac{y_2 - y_1}{x_2 - x_1} = \frac{1-2}{3-(-1)} = \frac{-1}{4}$ $or - 0.25$

PSAT Math Practice Test 2: Section 2

1) Choice C is correct

The amount of petrol consumed after x hours is: $6 \times x = 6x$, Petrol remaining after x hours driving: $80 - 6x$

2) Choice D is correct

Let x be the integer. Then: $3x - 12 = 120$, Add 12 both sides: $3x = 132$, Divide both sides by 3: $x = 44$

3) Choice B is correct

$$average \ (mean) = \frac{sum \ of \ terms}{number \ of \ terms} = \frac{9+12+15+16+19+16+14.5}{7} = 14.5$$

4) Choice B is correct

Use the formula of areas of circles. Area of a circle $= \pi r^2 \rightarrow 64 \, \pi = \pi r^2 \rightarrow 64 = r^2 \rightarrow r = 8$

Radius of the circle is 8. Now, use the circumference formula: Circumference $= 2\pi r = 2\pi \, (8) = 16 \, \pi$

5) Choice C is correct

$\begin{cases} x + 4y = 10 \\ 5x + 10y = 20 \end{cases} \rightarrow$ Multiply the top equation by -5 then,

$\begin{cases} -5x - 20y = -50 \\ 5x + 10y = 20 \end{cases} \rightarrow$ Add two equations

$-10y = -30 \rightarrow y = 3$, plug in the value of y into the first equation

$x + 4y = 10 \rightarrow x + 4(3) = 10 \rightarrow x + 12 = 10$

Subtract 12 from both sides of the equation. Then: $x + 12 = 10 \rightarrow x = -2$

6) Choice A is correct

$6b = 5a\sqrt{3} \rightarrow b = \frac{5a\sqrt{3}}{6}$, Therefore: $\frac{2b\sqrt{3}}{4a} = \frac{2 \times \frac{5a\sqrt{3}}{6} \times \sqrt{3}}{4a} = \frac{\frac{30a}{6}}{4a} = \frac{5a}{4a} = \frac{5}{4}$

7) Choice D is correct

$\dfrac{2}{5} \times 25 = \dfrac{50}{5} = 10$

8) Choice D is correct

The slop of line A is: $m = \frac{y_2 - y_1}{x_2 - x_1} = \frac{3-2}{4-3} = 1$, Parallel lines have the same slope and only choice D $(y = x)$ has slope of 1.

9) Choice A is correct

Line AB is the best fit line. Then, point $(6, 1)$ is the farthest from line AB.

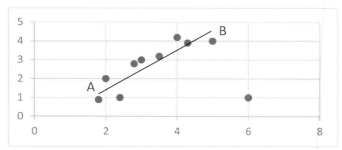

10) Choice B is correct

Choices A, C and D are incorrect because 80% of each of the numbers is non-whole number.

A. 49,   80% of $49 = 0.80 \times 49 = 39.2$

B. 35,   80% of $35 = 0.80 \times 35 = 28$

C. 12,   80% of $12 = 0.80 \times 12 = 9.6$

D. 32,   80% of $32 = 0.80 \times 32 = 25.6$

11) Choice A is correct

Let x be equal to 0.5, then: $x = 0.5$

$\sqrt{x^2 + 1} = \sqrt{0.5^2 + 1} = \sqrt{1.25} \approx 1.12$, $\sqrt{x^2} + 1 = \sqrt{0.5^2} + 1 = 0.5 + 1 = 1.5$

Then, option A is correct. $x < \sqrt{x^2 + 1} < \sqrt{x^2} + 1$

12) Choice C is correct

x is directly proportional to the square of y. Then: $x = cy^2$, $12 = c(2)^2 \rightarrow 12 = 4c \rightarrow c = \frac{12}{4} = 3$, The relationship between x and y is: $x = 3y^2$, $x = 75$, $75 = 3y^2 \rightarrow y^2 = \frac{75}{3} = 25 \rightarrow y = 5$

13) Choice D is correct

The amount of money that jack earns for one hour: $\frac{\$616}{44} = \$14$, Number of additional hours that he work to make enough money is: $\frac{\$826 - \$616}{1.5 \times \$14} = 10$, Number of total hours is: $44 + 10 = 54$

14) Choice C is correct

Let's find the mean (average), mode and median of the number of cities for each type of pollution. Number of cities for each type of pollution: $6, 3, 4, 9, 8$

$$average\ (mean) = \frac{sum\ of\ terms}{number\ of\ terms} = \frac{6+3+4+9+8}{5} = \frac{30}{5} = 6$$

Median is the number in the middle. To find median, first list numbers in order from smallest to largest. $3, 4, 6, 8, 9$, Median of the data is 6. Mode is the number which appears most often in a set of numbers. Therefore, there is no mode in the set of numbers.

Median = Mean, then, $a = c$

15) Choice A is correct

Percent of cities in the type of pollution A: $\frac{6}{10} \times 100 = 60\%$

Percent of cities in the type of pollution C: $\frac{4}{10} \times 100 = 40\%$

Percent of cities in the type of pollution D: $\frac{9}{10} \times 100 = 90\%$

16) Choice A is correct

Let the number of cities should be added to type of pollutions B be x. Then:

$\frac{x+3}{8} = 0.625 \rightarrow x + 3 = 8 \times 0.625 \rightarrow x + 3 = 5 \rightarrow x = 2$

17) Choice C is correct

The ratio of boy to girls is $4:7$. Therefore, there are 4 boys out of 11 students. To find the answer, first divide the total number of students by 11, then multiply the result by 4.

$44 \div 11 = 4 \Rightarrow 4 \times 4 = 16$, There are 16 boys and 28 $(44 - 16)$ girls. So, 12 more boys should be enrolled to make the ratio $1:1$

18) Choice A is correct

$AB = 12$ And $AC = 5$, $BC = \sqrt{12^2 + 5^2} = \sqrt{144 + 25} = \sqrt{169} = 13$

Perimeter $= 5 + 12 + 13 = 30$, Area $= \frac{5 \times 12}{2} = 5 \times 6 = 30$

In this case, the ratio of the perimeter of the triangle to its area is: $\frac{30}{30} = 1$

If the sides AB and AC become twice longer, then: $AB = 24$ And $AC = 10$

$BC = \sqrt{24^2 + 10^2} = \sqrt{576 + 100} = \sqrt{676} = 26$

Perimeter $= 26 + 24 + 10 = 60$, Area $= \frac{10 \times 24}{2} = 120$

In this case the ratio of the perimeter of the triangle to its area is: $\frac{60}{120} = \frac{1}{2}$

19) Choice D is correct

The capacity of a red box is 20% bigger than the capacity of a blue box and it can hold 30 books. Therefore, we want to find a number that 20% bigger than that number is 30. Let x be that number. Then: $1.20 \times x = 30$, Divide both sides of the equation by 1.2. Then:

$$x = \frac{30}{1.20} = 25$$

20) Choice C is correct

The smallest number is -15. To find the largest possible value of one of the other five integers, we need to choose the smallest possible integers for four of them. Let x be the largest number. Then: $-70 = (-15) + (-14) + (-13) + (-12) + (-11) + x \rightarrow -70 = -65 + x$

$\rightarrow x = -70 + 65 = -5$

21) Choice B is correct

Since $f(x)$ is linear function with a negative slop, then when $x = -2, f(x)$ is maximum and when $x = 3, f(x)$ is minimum. Then the ratio of the minimum value to the maximum value of the function is: $\frac{f(3)}{f(-2)} = \frac{-3(3)+1}{-3(-2)+1} = \frac{-8}{7} = -\frac{8}{7}$

22) Choice B is correct

Ratio of women to men in city A: $\frac{570}{600} = 0.95$

Ratio of women to men in city B: $\frac{291}{300} = 0.97$

Ratio of women to men in city C: $\frac{665}{700} = 0.95$

Ratio of women to men in city D: $\frac{528}{550} = 0.96$

23) Choice D is correct

Percentage of men in city A $= \frac{600}{1170} \times 100 = 51.28\%$

Percentage of women in city C $= \frac{665}{1365} \times 100 = 48.72\%$

Percentage of men in city A to percentage of women in city C $= \frac{51.28}{48.72} = 1.05$

24) Choice C is correct

Let the number of women should be added to city D be x, then:

$\frac{528 + x}{550} = 1.2 \rightarrow 528 + x = 550 \times 1.2 = 660 \rightarrow x = 132$

25) Choice C is correct

The perimeter of the rectangle is: $2x + 2y = 30 \rightarrow x + y = 15 \rightarrow x = 15 - y$

The area of the rectangle is: $x \times y = 50 \rightarrow (15 - y)(y) = 50 \rightarrow y^2 - 15y + 50 = 0$

Solve the quadratic equation by factoring method.

$(y - 5)(y - 10) = 0 \rightarrow y = 5$ (Unacceptable, because y must be greater than 5) or $y = 10$

If $y = 10 \rightarrow x \times y = 50 \rightarrow x \times 10 = 50 \rightarrow x = 5$

26) Choice D is correct

$$\sin \beta = \frac{opposit\ side}{hypotenuse}$$

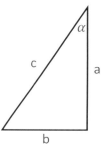

To find the hypotenuse, we need to use Pythagorean theorem.

$a^2 + b^2 = c^2 \rightarrow c = \sqrt{a^2 + b^2}$, $\sin(\beta) = \frac{b}{c} = \frac{b}{\sqrt{a^2+b^2}}$

27) Choice C is correct

$\left|\frac{x}{2} - 2x + 10\right| < 5 \rightarrow \left|-\frac{3}{2}x + 10\right| < 5 \rightarrow -5 < -\frac{3}{2}x + 10 < 5$

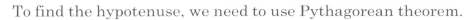

Subtract 10 from all sides of the inequality.

$\rightarrow -5 - 10 < -\frac{3}{2}x + 10 - 10 < 5 - 10 \rightarrow -15 < -\frac{3}{2}x < -5$

Multiply all sides by 2. $\rightarrow 2 \times (-15) < 2 \times \left(-\frac{3x}{2}\right) < 2 \times (-5) \rightarrow -30 < -3x < -10$

Divide all sides by -3. (Remember that when you divide all sides of an inequality by a negative number, the inequality sing will be swapped. $<$ becomes $>$)

$\rightarrow \frac{-30}{-3} > \frac{-3x}{-3} > \frac{-10}{-3}, \rightarrow 10 > x > \frac{10}{3} \rightarrow \frac{10}{3} < x < 10$

28) The answer is 1.

The intersection of two functions is the point with 2 for x. Then:

$f(2) = g(2)$ and $g(2) = (2 \times (2)) - 3 = 4 - 3 = 1$

Then, $f(2) = 1 \rightarrow a(2)^2 + b(2) + c = 1 \rightarrow 4a + 2b + c = 1$ (i)

The value of x in the vertex of the parabola is: $x = -\frac{b}{2a} \rightarrow -2 = -\frac{b}{2a} \rightarrow b = 4a$ (ii)

In the point $(-2, 5)$, the value of the $f(x)$ is 5.

$f(-2) = 5 \rightarrow a(-2)^2 + b(-2) + c = 5 \rightarrow 4a - 2b + c = 5$ (iii)

Using the first two equations:

$\begin{cases} 4a + 2b + c = 1 \\ 4a - 2b + c = 5 \end{cases} \rightarrow$

Equation 1 minus equation 2 is: (i)−(iii) $\rightarrow 4b = -4 \rightarrow b = -1$ (iv)

Plug in the value of b in the second equation: $b = 4a \rightarrow a = \frac{b}{4} = -\frac{1}{4}$

Plug in the values of a and be in the first equation. Then:

$\rightarrow 4\left(\frac{-1}{4}\right) + 2(-1) + c = 1 \rightarrow -1 - 2 + c = 1 \rightarrow c = 1 + 3 \rightarrow c = 4$

the product of a, b and $c = \left(-\frac{1}{4}\right) \times (-1) \times 4 = 1$

29) The answer is 60.

The relationship among all sides of special right triangle

$30° - 60° - 90°$ is provided in this triangle:

In this triangle, the opposite side of 30° angle is half of the hypotenuse.

Draw the shape of this question: The ladder is the hypotenuse. Therefore, the ladder is 60 ft.

30) The answer is 3.

Let x be the length of an edge of cube, then the volume of a cube is: $V = x^3$

The surface area of cube is: $SA = 6x^2$, The volume of cube A is $\frac{1}{2}$ of its surface area. Then: $x^3 = \frac{6x^2}{2} \rightarrow x^3 = 3x^2$, divide both side of the equation by x^2. Then: $\frac{x^3}{x^2} = \frac{3x^2}{x^2} \rightarrow x = 3$

31) The answer is 5.

$3x + 6y = \frac{-3y^2 + 15}{x}$, Multiply both sides by x.

$x \times (3x + 6y) = x \times \left(\frac{-3y^2 + 15}{x}\right) \rightarrow 3x^2 + 6xy = -3y^2 + 15$

$\rightarrow 3x^2 + 6xy + 3y^2 = 15 \rightarrow 3 \times (x^2 + 2xy + y^2) = 15 \rightarrow x^2 + 2xy + y^2 = \frac{15}{3}$

$x^2 + 2xy + y^2 = (x + y)^2$, Then: $\rightarrow (x + y)^2 = 5$

www.EffortlessMath.com

... So Much More Online!

- ❖ FREE Math lessons

- ❖ More Math learning books!

- ❖ Mathematics Worksheets

- ❖ Online Math Tutors

Need a PDF version of this book?

Visit www.EffortlessMath.com

Receive the PDF version of this book or get another FREE book!

Thank you for using our Book!

Do you LOVE this book?

Then, you can get the PDF version of this book or another book absolutely FREE!

Please email us at:

info@EffortlessMath.com

for details.

Author's Final Note

I hope you enjoyed reading this book. You've made it through the book! Great job!

First of all, thank you for purchasing this study guide. I know you could have picked any number of books to help you prepare for your PSAT Math test, but you picked this book and for that I am extremely grateful.

It took me years to write this study guide for the PSAT Math because I wanted to prepare a comprehensive PSAT Math study guide to help test takers make the most effective use of their valuable time while preparing for the test.

After teaching and tutoring PSAT math for over a decade, I've gathered my personal notes and lessons to develop this study guide. It is my greatest hope that the lessons in this book could help you prepare for your test successfully.

If you have any questions, please contact me at reze@effortlessmath.com and I will be glad to assist. Your feedback will help me to greatly improve the quality of my books in the future and make this book even better. Furthermore, I expect that I have made a few minor errors somewhere in this study guide. If you think this to be the case, please let me know so I can fix the issue as soon as possible.

If you enjoyed this book and found some benefit in reading this, I'd like to hear from you and hope that you could take a quick minute to post a review on the book's Amazon page. To leave your valuable feedback, please visit: amzn.to/37K4jtD

Or scan this QR code.

I personally go over every single review, to make sure my books really are reaching out and helping students and test takers. Please help me help PSAT Math test takers, by leaving a review!

I wish you all the best in your future success!

Reza Nazari

Math teacher and author

Made in the USA
Columbia, SC
23 April 2022